Theories of Comparative Analysis

Theories of Comparative Analysis

Daniel S. Weld

The MIT Press
Cambridge, Massachusetts
London, England

© 1990 Massachusetts Institute of Technology

All rights reserved. No part of this book may be reproduced in any form by any electronic or mechanical means (including photocopying, recording, or information storage and retrieval) without permission in writing from the publisher.

This book was set in Century Schoolbook and printed and bound in the United States of America.

Library of Congress Number: 90-52608
Further Library of Congress Cataloging-in-Publication data is available.

*To my parents and my senior sibling
Anne, Philip and Kathy*

Contents

	List of Figures	xi
	Series Foreword	xiii
	Acknowledgments	xv
	Preface	xvii
1	Introduction	1
1.1	Reader's Guide	3
1.2	Motivation	4
	1.2.1 Why Qualitative Physics?	4
	1.2.2 Why Comparative Analysis?	7
1.3	Context	8
	1.3.1 Qualitative Values	8
	1.3.2 Ontologies for Modeling Change	10
	1.3.3 Qualitative Simulation	12
	1.3.4 Types of Comparative Analysis	14
1.4	Differential Qualitative Analysis	15
	1.4.1 Perspectives	15
	1.4.2 Changes in Behavioral Topology	19
1.5	Exaggeration	20
	1.5.1 Transform, Simulate, and Scale Phases	20
	1.5.2 Qualitative Hyperreal Representation	23
	1.5.3 Persistence and Arrival Filtering	25
1.6	Conclusions	27
2	Differential Qualitative Analysis	29
2.1	Preliminaries	29
	2.1.1 Qualitative Behavior	30
	2.1.2 Comparing Two Behaviors	31
	2.1.3 Comparing Two Behaviors over Intervals	33
	2.1.4 Time as a Perspective	35
2.2	DQ Inference Rules	35
	2.2.1 Duration Rule	36
	2.2.2 Derivative Rules	39

		2.2.3 Perspective Rules	42
		2.2.4 Constants	43
		2.2.5 Rules with Time as a Perspective	44
		2.2.6 Rules from Qualitative Arithmetic	44
	2.3	Implementation	45
	2.4	Extensions for Diagnosis	48
	2.5	Changes in Behavioral Topology	49
		2.5.1 Initial Behavior Inconsistent	52
		2.5.2 Finding Other Consistent Behaviors	58
	2.6	Summary	60
3		Exaggeration	61
	3.1	Qualitative Representation Extensions	62
		3.1.1 The Hyperreal Numbers	62
		3.1.2 The Qualitative Hyperreals	64
		3.1.3 Behaviors over Hyperreal Time	66
	3.2	Transform Phase	67
		3.2.1 Choice of Parameter	67
		3.2.2 Choice of Direction	69
		3.2.3 Choice of Distance	70
	3.3	Simulate Phase	72
		3.3.1 How QSIM Works	73
		3.3.2 Transition Tables	74
		3.3.3 Constraint Filters	82
		3.3.4 Predecessor-Persistence Filter	84
		3.3.5 Successor-Arrival Filter	89
		3.3.6 Improving the Temporal Filters	93
		3.3.7 Irrelevant-Transition Filter	96
		3.3.8 Summary	97
	3.4	Scale Phase	98
		3.4.1 Scaling Durations	99
		3.4.2 Multiple Behaviors	102
	3.5	Summary	103

4	Analysis of Techniques	105
4.1	Similarities and Shared Problems	105
	4.1.1 Ambiguous Questions	105
	4.1.2 Qualitative Arithmetic is Ambiguous	105
	4.1.3 Linearity is not Represented	107
4.2	Theoretical Difference	109
	4.2.1 Predicting Partial Derivatives	109
	4.2.2 Predicting Asymptotes	111
4.3	Competence Difference	112
	4.3.1 Weaknesses of Exaggeration	112
	4.3.2 Weaknesses of DQ Analysis	113
4.4	Performance Difference	116
	4.4.1 DQ Analysis is Polynomial	117
	4.4.2 Exaggeration is Exponential	118
4.5	Explanation Difference	119
	4.5.1 What Makes a Good Explanation?	120
	4.5.2 Exaggeration can Produce Simpler Answers	122
	4.5.3 Unnatural Explanations	123
4.6	Combining the Techniques	125
5	Related Work	127
5.1	Sensitivity Analysis	127
5.2	Williams' Temporal Representation	128
5.3	de Kleer's IQ Analysis	129
5.4	Forbus' DQ Analysis	130
5.5	Raiman's FOG	130
5.6	Kuipers' Time Scale Abstraction	132
5.7	Davis' CHEPACHET	133
6	Conclusions	137
6.1	Summary	137

6.2	Future Work		137
	6.2.1 Augmenting DQ Analysis		138
	6.2.2 Other Uses for Exaggeration		138
	6.2.3 Reasoning about Discontinuous Systems		139
	6.2.4 Reasoning with Multiple Models		140
	6.2.5 Mixed Qualitative Quantitative Reasoning		142
6.3	Conclusions		142
A	Glossary		145
B	A Useful Example		151
C	Readings in Nonstandard Analysis		153
D	HR-QSIM Transition Tables		155
E	Program Output for the Spring and Block		159
F	List of Examples Implemented		167
	Bibliography		179
	Index		183

List of Figures

1.1	Ideal Spring Attached to Block on Frictionless Table	2
1.2	Appropriate Plate Model Depends on Context	6
1.3	Overview of the DQ Analysis Algorithm	16
1.4	QSIM Behavior for Stable Spring Oscillation	17
1.5	Actual Plot of Force versus Time	18
1.6	Hot Oil Flows Through Heat Exchanger	20
1.7	Initial Behavior of Heat Exchanger	21
1.8	Perturbed Behavior of Heat Exchanger	22
1.9	Overview of the Exaggeration Algorithm	23
1.10	Some Values in the Heat Hyperreal Quantity Space	24
2.1	$P\Uparrow_{(0,1)}^{X} \ yet P\|_{(0,1)}^{Y} \ and P\Downarrow_{(0,1)}^{Z}$	39
2.2	Propositions Are Encoded Directly Into ARK Rules	46
2.3	CA Generated Explanation for Increasing the Mass in the Spring/Block System	48
2.4	Overview of the DQ Analysis Algorithm	50
2.5	QSIM State Tree Generates Possible Behaviors	52
2.6	The Initial Behavior Corresponds to the Path (QS1, QS2, QS3)	53
2.7	The Behavior Corresponding to the Path (QS1, QS2, QS5, QS6, QS7)	55
3.1	Overview of the Exaggeration Algorithm	62
3.2	Regular and Counter Flow Heat Exchangers	68
3.3	Transform Phase Output	71
3.4	A Boiler	72
3.5	Transitions among Standard (QSIM) Qualitative Values	76
3.6	QSIM Transition for (l_i, std)	77
3.7	Transitions among Qualitative Hyperreal Values	79
3.8	Hyperreal Transitions from (l_i, std)	80
3.9	Hyperreal Transitions from $((\text{HALO} \ 0 \ +), (inc \ negl))$	80
3.10	The Difference Between Peristence and Arrival Times	85

3.11	The Distance-Rate-Time Table	87
3.12	Behavior of a Standard Heat Exchanger	99
3.13	Behavior of an Infinite Flow Rate Heat Exchanger	100
3.14	Temporal Addition	101
4.1	Exaggeration Approximates a Curve with a Line through an Asymptote	111
4.2	Nonmonotonic Systems can Fool Exaggeration	113
4.3	Equilibrium State for Pumped Containers	115
4.4	A Sample Rule	118

Series Foreword

Artificial intelligence is the study of intelligence using the ideas and methods of computation. Unfortunately, a definition of intelligence seems impossible at the moment because intelligence appears to be an amalgam of so many information-processing and information-representation abilities.

Of course psychology, philosophy, linguistics, and related disciplines offer various perspectives and methodologies for studying intelligence. For the most part, however, the theories proposed in these fields are too incomplete and too vaguely stated to be realized in computational terms. Something more is needed, even though valuable ideas, relationships, and constraints can be gleaned from traditional studies of what are, after all, impressive existence proofs that intelligence is in fact possible.

Artificial intelligence offers a new perspective and a new methodology. Its central goal is to make computers intelligent, both to make them more useful and to understand the principles that make intelligence possible. That intelligent computers will be extremely useful is obvious. The more profound point is that artificial intelligence aims to understand intelligence using the ideas and methods of computation, thus offering a radically new and different basis for theory formation. Most of the people doing work in artificial intelligence believe that these theories will apply to any intelligent information processor, whether biological or solid state.

There are side effects that deserve attention, too. Any program that will successfully model even a small part of intelligence will be inherently massive and complex. Consequently, artificial intelligence continually confronts the limits of computer-science technology. The problems encountered have been hard enough and interesting enough to seduce artificial intelligence people into working on them with enthusiasm. It is natural, then, that there has been a steady flow of ideas from artificial intelligence to computer science, and the flow shows no sign of abating.

The purpose of The MIT Press Series in Artificial Intelligence is to provide people in many areas, both professionals and students, with timely, detailed information about what is happening on the frontiers in research centers all over the world.

Patrick Henry Winston
J. Michael Brady
Daniel Bobrow

Acknowledgments

This book is a revised version of my Ph.D. dissertation written at the Artificial Intelligence Laboratory of the Massachusetts Institute of Technology.[1] Tomas Lozano-Perez, my supervisor, was a major inspiration; I hope I can develop his taste and judgement in research. The rest of my committee were equally helpful. Johan de Kleer's sharp imagination and blunt criticism taught me what was important about qualitative physics. Randy Davis helped me distinguish important themes from mechanisms and taught me how to explain. Patrick Winston showed me how to present my work.

Ken Forbus introduced me to qualitative physics and gave many useful suggestions. Pat Hayes made research fun and was always game for a fierce argument. Ernie Davis made many helpful suggestions, including a proof of proposition 14 and substantial contributions to the proofs of proposition 20 and 17. David McAllester helped prove proposition 3. Ben Kuipers provided QSIM, facilitating both my theories and implementations, and many helpful suggestions. Most important was the comradery close to home; Mark Shirley and Brian Williams were exceptional companions and critics who endured my ramblings and taught me much.

Both the broad directions and technical details of my work were influenced by discussions with and comments from Marty Tennenbaum, Narinder Singh, Reid Simmons, Jeff Shrager, Paul Resnick, John Mohammed, Jerry Roylance, Mike Lowry, Glenn Kramer, Dan Huttenlocher, Paul Horwitz, Steve Hanks, Walter Hamscher, Jay Freeman, Gary Drescher, Dave Chapman, Dan Carnese, John Seely Brown, Harry Barrow, Steve Bagley, and Phil Agre. The HT, 7AI and girlscouts define my memories of MIT. Thanks to all my MIT friends; I will miss you.

Margaret, fortunately, I need not miss; she gave me the reason to finish. However, it was my family that *started* me on this whole education adventure. Thus it is to them that I owe the biggest debt.

---

[1] Support for the laboratory's artificial intelligence research is provided in part by the Advanced Research Projects Agency of the Department of Defense under Office of Naval Research contract N00014-85-K-0124. Portions of this research were done at the Xerox Palo Alto Research Center, at Schlumberger CAS Palo Alto Research, and at the Department of Computer Science and Engineering at the University of Washington and were funded in part by National Science Foundation grants IRI-8902010 and IRI-8957302.

Preface

The ability to understand and adapt the physical world to fit varying needs is one hallmark of intelligence. Our knowledge of the physical sciences, from Newtonian mechanics to quantum electrodynamics, is in large part responsible for our success at manipulating the environment, just as our failure to fully comprehend the complex interconnection of our ecosystem may lead us to global disaster.

Artificial intelligence research on automated reasoning about physical systems is important for several reasons. First, it may allow robots to predict the effects of their actions on a dynamic world. Second, it may lead to powerful tools for automated design, diagnosis, and monitoring of complex systems such as electronic circuits or chemical plants. Third, it may enable the construction of algorithms that generate causal descriptions explaining how physical systems work; these algorithms could be used in intelligent tutoring systems or in an electronic encyclopedia. Finally, research into qualitative physics, as the field is commonly called, may yield techniques that provide new insights into the functioning of complex systems whose behavior is currently mysterious.

This book describes recent progress in the automation of one form of reasoning: comparative analysis confronts the problem of predicting how a system will react to perturbations in its parameters, and explaining why. For example, comparative analysis could be asked to explain why the period of an oscillating spring/block system would increase if the mass of the block were larger. In this book, I formalize the task of comparative analysis and present two solution techniques: differential qualitative (DQ) analysis and exaggeration. Both techniques solve many comparative analysis problems, providing explanations suitable for use by design systems, automated diagnosticians, intelligent tutoring systems, and algorithms performing explanation based generalization.

This book explains the theoretical basis for each technique, describes how each is implemented, and discusses the differences between the two. DQ analysis is sound: it never generates an incorrect answer to a comparative analysis question. And while exaggeration does occasionally produce misleading answers, it solves a larger class of problems than DQ analysis and generates simpler explanations.

We are still far from knowing how to build programs that display the breadth of understanding of a college physics student, much less a skilled semiconductor designer or biochemistry researcher. Yet the techniques of DQ analysis and exaggeration advance the reasoning capabilities of today's computers and pave the way for the continuing development of tools that will help us understand the effects, both good and bad, of changes to our environment.

Theories of Comparative Analysis

1 Introduction

The problem of symbolic analysis of real-world systems is central to many problems in artificial intelligence. For example, robots that can interact with a changing world, programs that can design electronic circuits, and systems that aid in medical diagnosis all need a comprehensive understanding of their environment. They must be able to analyze their surroundings and evaluate the effects of their actions. Qualitative representations are often appropriate for this analysis because they suppress irrelevant detail and highlight the fundamental processes that are present. For example, rather than representing the pressure of water in a pipe by a real number, it is often sufficient to know its ordinal relation to important landmark values like the pressure that will cause the pipe to rupture.

Recently, considerable emphasis has been put on a specific kind of analysis: qualitative simulation [11, 21, 69, 38, 64]. Qualitative simulation seeks to produce a description of a system's behavior over time. This description often takes the form of a tree of histories recording the system's qualitatively interesting changes over time [72].

This book discusses the problem of comparative analysis, a task that is the complement of qualitative simulation. Whereas qualitative simulation takes a structural description of a system and predicts its behavior, comparative analysis takes as input this behavior and a perturbation and outputs a description of how and why the behavior would change as a result of the perturbation.

For example, given an ideal spring attached to a block on a frictionless table (figure 1.1), a qualitative simulator would say that the block would first move one direction, then stop, then reverse, etc. A description of oscillation would result. Comparative analysis, on the other hand, takes this description of oscillation and evaluates the effects of perturbations. For example, it would deduce that the period of oscillation would lengthen if the mass of the block were increased, and explain why. Just as qualitative simulation works without explicit equations for the value of each parameter as a function of time, comparative analysis does not need a formula for the period of oscillation.

The most important result of comparative analysis is the explanation of *why* the behavior changes, since explanations can not be generated by symbolic or numeric solution of a differential equation model. This book presents two techniques for solving comparative analysis problems: differential qualitative (DQ) analysis and exaggeration. Both techniques

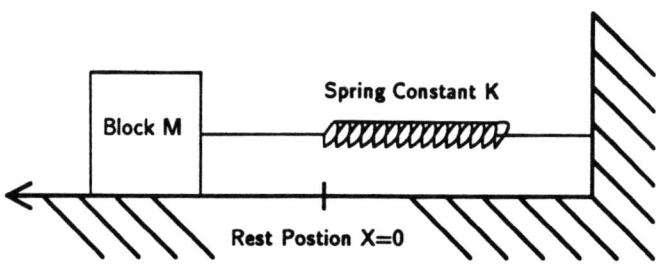

Figure 1.1
Ideal Spring Attached to Block on Frictionless Table

have been implemented and have a solid theoretical foundations, yet they perform differently and generate different kinds of explanations. For example, DQ analysis would explain that the block would have a longer period if the mass were increased:

> Since force is inversely proportional to position, the force on the block will remain the same when the mass is increased. But if the block is heavier, then it won't accelerate as fast. So it will always be moving slower. Thus the block will take longer to complete a full period (assuming it travels the same distance).

Exaggeration answers the same question in a completely different manner:

> If the mass were infinite, then the block would hardly budge. Thus the period would be infinite. So increasing the mass even a smaller amount should cause the period to increase as well.

This book explores the differences and relative advantages of the two approaches. The basic conclusions are the following:

Differential qualitative analysis and exaggeration are complementary techniques for comparative analysis. DQ analysis always answers correctly while exaggeration can make false predictions on two classes of questions. However, exaggeration solves a wider variety of problems than does DQ analysis. As a result, the two techniques reinforce each other and solve many comparative analysis problems.

This thesis is argued by a description of each technique, by empirical tests using computer implementations, and by a theoretical analysis explaining why they perform differently.

1.1 Reader's Guide

The rest of this introduction gives an overview of the book. Sections 1.2.1 and 1.2.2 are motivational; they explain why qualitative physics is interesting in the context of AI, and why comparative analysis is interesting in the context of qualitative physics. Section 1.3 presents the context for this work; this should be helpful for those readers unfamiliar with the concepts of qualitative value, ontology, and qualitative simulation. In addition this section describes the range of possible comparative analysis techniques. The next two sections summarize the intuition behind the two comparative analysis. Section 1.4 introduces the main points of DQ analysis: perspectives, inference rules using relative change values, and changes in behavioral topology. The next section discusses exaggeration and explains how it is composed of three phases: transform, simulate, and scale. Finally, section 1.6 summarizes the similarities and differences between the two approaches and suggests a hybrid architecture that takes best advantage of the strengths of each technique.

The rest of the book presents the details of the two comparative analysis theories. Chapter 2 explains DQ analysis starting with a formal definition of relative change and perspectives. Next these concepts are used to specify numerous inference rules, all of which are proven sound. These inference rules are the essence of DQ analysis. The chapter explains how a simple constraint propagator applies the rules in forward-chaining fashion to solve numerous comparative analysis problems.

Chapter 3 presents the details of exaggeration starting with the qualitative hyperreal representation used to describe systems with exaggerated perturbations (like the block with infinite mass). The chapter describes all three phases of the exaggeration algorithm: transform, simulate, and scale, but the emphasis is on the simulate phase due to the technical difficulty of simulation using the qualitative hyperreal representation.

Chapter 4 analyzes the DQ and exaggeration techniques by comparing them along several dimensions. Unlike the previous chapters, which may be read independently after finishing the introduction, chapter 4 is best appreciated after completing previous chapters; see [66] for a self-contained analysis. Chapter 5 is a discussion of related work, and chapter 6 concludes the book with a summary and suggestions for future research.

Unfortunately, the technical portions of this book contain a considerable amount of mathematical definitions and jargon. To ease this burden on the reader, appendix A contains a glossary for quick reference. Appendix E contains the actual input and sample runs of the DQ analysis and exaggeration programs. Appendix F records the performance of the DQ analysis and exaggeration implementations on more than fifty comparative analysis problems pertaining to twenty system models.

1.2 Motivation

Before delving deeply into the technical details of comparative analysis techniques, or even the larger field of qualitative reasoning about physical systems, it is worth considering the relevance of these areas to larger problems in artificial intelligence.

1.2.1 Why Qualitative Physics?

The goal of qualitative physics is to make explicit the unspoken intuition of experts in the physical sciences [68]. I distinguish qualitative physics from the field of naive physics. Qualitative physics is interested in expert reasoning, not in duplicating the common mistakes of novices. Qualitative physics may also be distinguished from other research on common sense reasoning. Although qualitative physics deductions indeed seem like common sense to those who perform them, the techniques are not obvious. Most people do not correctly solve qualitative physics problems without some training.

1.2. Motivation

Although physics and engineering classes concentrate on teaching techniques for manipulating and solving equations, considerable expertise is necessary to correctly choose appropriate equations to solve in the first place. Decisions regarding appropriate quantitative models of a system are frequently based on qualitative information and analysis, such as a qualitative expectation of the system's behavior over time. In fact many physics problems can be solved by strictly qualitative means. If a problem specification is lacking complete numerical information, then qualitative physics may be the only method for obtaining an answer. If the goal is a qualitative understanding of the system's behavior, then partial information is perfectly appropriate. One doesn't need to know the exact mass of the block in figure 1.1 to deduce that an oscillation will result. A person would be considered rather slow if he refused to make this prediction until being informed of the 1.5 kilogram value.

Another type of qualitative physics decision, the choice of model for a system, can make a huge difference to problem solving performance. Early systems for analog circuit design, such as SYN [13], attempted to calculate circuit parameters by propagating constraints using the obvious algebraic equations (all possible applications of Kirchhoff's Current Law, etc.). Using Macsyma's algebraic manipulation subroutines [42], SYN generated intermediate subexpressions that were much more complex than those used by a trained engineer, or even by a sophisticated student. De Kleer's successor programs, QUAL [9] and EQUAL [10], improved on SYN by exploiting the qualitative knowledge and expectations of an engineer, using simplified models of devices that drastically facilitate reasoning when appropriate. Because this research was grounded in the domain of electronics, his results have not received as much attention as they deserve. Hopefully, the following simple mechanical example will make the point.

Consider a rectangular plate fabricated of thin steel. This simple structure could function in many capacities: as a weight, damper, spring, or even as part of a capacitor. Now consider the problem of automatically analyzing devices built of metal plates (and other simple components). For example, consider the two devices in figure 1.2 — the only difference between them is a ninety-degree rotation in the orientation of the metal plate. Since we know equations for modeling gravitational attraction, damping, capacitance, et cetera, the obvious approach would be to have our program generate all possible equations for each device

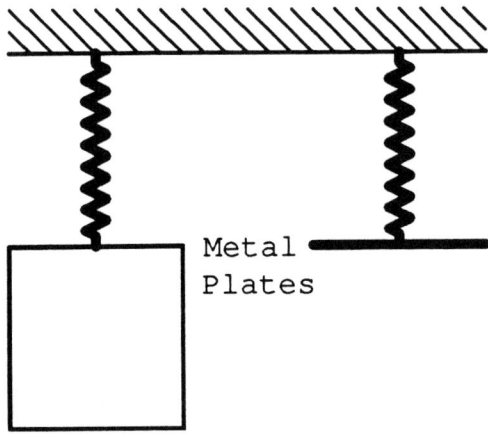

Figure 1.2
Appropriate Plate Model Depends on Context

and send them off to an algebraic solver.

But this would be terribly silly. Simple inspection of figure 1.2 shows that gravitational attraction due to the mass of both plates is relevant, but damping due to air friction is probably only important to the device on the right. In neither case is the spring-like behavior of the plates of interest; nor are capacitive effects relevant. Determining an appropriate model for a system is one of the principle goals of qualitative physics; however, it is not easy. While the example above demonstrates that qualitative methods typically suffice, mechanical devices often require complex geometric reasoning which appears easy for people yet difficult for computers. Hence, the greatest progress to date has been achieved by encoding the intuitions of electrical engineers, for example by EQUAL [10] and Slices [61]. Recent progress has also been made in the domain of thermodynamic systems — SCHISM [59] solves textbook thermodynamic problems by performing qualitative simulation to recognize the teleology of the system and focus the equation-generation process.

An understanding of how humans reason effectively about complex physical systems would have many uses. A theory of the knowledge used in qualitative physics would make it much easier to train people to perform as experts. In addition, qualitative physics programs could

1.2. Motivation

explain their reasoning with "causal arguments" [26] formed from the dependencies recorded by constraint propagation algorithms. The resulting intelligent tutoring systems could teach physics and engineering more effectively. Qualitative physics also forms the foundation for model-based theories of design [71] and diagnosis [6, 15, 7].

Besides its immediate application, work on qualitative physics has an impact on a more general study of intelligence. Since any thorough investigation into the structure of knowledge and reasoning in a domain is likely to reveal issues that apply to other domains as well, one might as well select a domain based on the expected ease of progress. Compared to most any other area, the domain of simple physical devices is easier to codify.

1.2.2 Why Comparative Analysis?

Comparative analysis, the qualitative analog of sensitivity analysis, is the problem of determining how and why the behavior of a system will change when its structure is changed. Even more important than the prediction of the direction of change is comparative analysis' explanation of why the change will occur. Many artificial intelligence goals, including automated design, diagnosis, and intelligent tutoring systems, require comparative analysis as an important component; the explanation is used in many different ways.

- One method of automated design is the principled modification of previous designs [71]. For example, suppose a library design for a VLSI pullup circuit has too long a rise time. If the problem solver considers increasing the width of some wire to decrease the rise time, it would like to know the ramifications of this modification *relative to the initial behavior*. Will the delay decrease? What happens to power dissipation? Comparative analysis answers these questions, in qualitative terms, as is appropriate for initial design evaluation. By analyzing an explanation of why the changes happen, the problem solver could then focus on further changes to counteract undesired effects.

- Many of the programs which perform diagnosis from first principles use generate and test paradigms [27]. Comparative analysis can simplify the diagnosis of continuous systems (such as analog electronic devices) in two ways. Comparative analysis provides a direct test for certain hypothesized faults; if one suspects that a resistor has a low value, comparative analysis can predict the resulting circuit behavior. If this prediction does not match the observed behavior, the generator might use the explanation to suggest or rule out additional candidate faults.

- A key subproblem of intelligent tutoring systems (ITS) is the automatic explanation of the behavior of complex systems. Most AI work in this direction has focused on the role of qualitative simulation when explaining a device's mechanism, i.e., how the device achieves its function [62, 26]. Qualitative simulation is a critical component of explanation generation, but understanding how systems respond to changes is also important. One doesn't really understand the workings of a refrigerator if one can't explain the effect of a stronger compressor on its efficiency and minimum temperature.

While this book may be viewed as a detailed investigation of the comparative analysis problem, it can also be seen in a more general light. The analysis of the relative merits of DQ analysis and exaggeration exposes issues and tradeoffs that apply to all of qualitative physics and model-based reasoning. Through a careful study of comparative analysis, much is learned about the soundness / completeness dichotomy, the importance of modeling in model-based reasoning, and the fundamental limitations of qualitative arithmetic.

1.3 Context

The research described in this book builds on the work of a large number of people. By summarizing that foundation, this section provides the general background that the rest of the book requires. Unlike chapter 5, which describes related work in a more detailed and technical fashion, this section is quite general and concerns all of qualitative physics.

1.3.1 Qualitative Values

Traditionally, physical systems have been described with real numbers and continuous functions of time. The first researchers seeking a discrete or qualitative representation discovered that there were many possibilities. The first attempts at qualitative representations were motivated by

1.3. Context

linguistic variables. In other words, rather than representing the temperature of water by a real number signifying degrees Celsius, the symbols WARM, HOT, and VERY-HOT could be used. However, linguistic variables turned out to be inappropriate for qualitative reasoning because they were arbitrary. Unless the different values (i.e., HOT and VERY-HOT) correspond to important distinctions, the symbolic representation is an encumbrance rather than a help.

The secret in choosing a good set of qualitative values is identifying the relevant distinctions. In other words, it is impossible to divorce the choice of representation from the kind of reasoning one is trying to automate. If the goal is to build a program that will reason about fluid flow through copper pipes, then the natural distinctions might be whether the temperature is below the freezing point or above the boiling point. Forbus first coined the term QUANTITY SPACE for a representation based on ordinal relations[1] to important LANDMARK VALUES such as the boiling and freezing temperatures [21]. In this work on Qualitative Process (QP) theory, Forbus suggested that one could choose a set of landmark points by considering the values where processes (such as freezing) started or stopped. This clearly satisfies the relevancy criterion since processes cause significant change (such as breaking one's pipes!).

The most common quantity space is that produced by the sole landmark value zero and yielding three qualitative values that are commonly written $(minf, 0)$, 0, and $(0, inf)$.[2] These values are particularly useful when describing the derivative of a quantity since they correspond to situations in which the quantity is increasing, decreasing or steady. Frequently, this simple information is sufficient to support a number of conclusions about a system's behavior — especially in an electronics domain.

Of course, the quantity space representation is no panacea. Since qualitative values contain less information than real numbers, some trains of reasoning result in ambiguity. Often this ambiguity matches people's intuitions about a situation. For example, suppose a faucet is pouring water into a leaky bucket; without more information, it is impossible to determine if the bucket's water level will increase, decrease or stay constant. That information might be qualitative (an inequality relation between the pouring and leaking flow rates) or quantitative (real values

---

[1] Ordinal relations are the simple inequalities: less than, equal to, or greater than.
[2] A common alternative notation uses the symbols $[-]$, $[0]$, and $[+]$.

for the two quantities). In general, however, quantitative information is necessary to eliminate the chance of any ambiguity. This is due to the weakness of the algebraic operations that can be defined on a qualitative value space (section 4.1). Various approaches have been developed to ameliorate this problem: handling special cases [17, 18], integrating quantitative information [74], and introducing new qualitative distinctions as needed [36, 38].

1.3.2 Ontologies for Modeling Change

According to Webster, one definition of "ontology" is "A particular theory about being or reality." In qualitative physics, the term takes on the more specialized meaning of a conceptual framework for modeling objects in the world and causes of change. To date, three major ontologies have been proposed: device, process and constraint [23]. Each of these choices has a unique set of advantages and disadvantages.

The device ontology [11, 69] is based on the theory of system dynamics [56]. The basic idea is to view a physical system as a collection of devices (such as resistors and capacitors) connected in a fixed topology. The behavior of each class of devices is specified by a set of rules relating values at the different ports of the device to each other. For example, resistors might be declared to have two ports, and a rule might specify that the difference in voltage between the two ports must be equal to the current flowing through the resistor times a constant unique to the resistor (Ohm's law). Just as devices represent idealized primitive components, connections between the ports of two devices represent idealized wires. The device ontology has two major advantages: the ontology's fixed topology allows efficient, local computation, and the solid foundation of system dynamics facilitates the generation of qualitative models. As may be inferred from the example, the device ontology is very popular for representing electronic circuits. While the framework is certainly not limited to that domain, the ontology is especially suitable for electronics because of the close correspondence between the idealized device-models of electrical components and their actual behavior. In other domains the device ontology is not quite as popular because of the difficulty in choosing a suitable device model; see for example, figure 1.2. In addition, in many domains it is difficult to think of the world as composed of discrete, lumped-parameter devices. For example, it would be unnatural to model a pot of water on a stove burner with the device ontology. To

1.3. Context

quote Forbus:

> We can consider the water in the pot ... to be an object. If the water boils, this object will decrease in size until it vanishes. It is hard to think of this system as a collection of devices, since the reasoning requires "clipping" a device out of the network when the water vanishes. Such changes in the network topology lie outside the device formalism ([23, page 265]).

The process ontology (exemplified by qualitative process (QP) theory [21]) was developed to model systems in which there is no fixed topology of interaction and in which the set of objects in existence changes as time progresses. Intuitively, a process is something that causes objects to change over time. For example, in the example above, heat flow and boiling would be represented as processes. One of the main differences between the device and process ontologies lies in how the qualitative equations governing legal behaviors are generated. In the device ontology these equations are provided directly by the device models. In the process ontology, however, these equations must be constructed dynamically at run time by a rather complex procedure. Each process can directly influence a set of quantities, and these quantities may be influenced by more than one process. The equations that determine how these quantities will change over time are formed by summing the influences of the various processes and applying a closed-world assumption. In addition, some quantities may be indirectly influenced; in this case, the equations are formed by summing over a different set of laws associated with objects and other processes. The process ontology provides a very flexible framework for modeling the world, but the cost of this flexibility is computational inefficiency. Since the set of processes and objects in existence can change over time, the procedure that constructs the equations must run repeatedly. While sophisticated implementation techniques have dramatically increased the speed of process-ontology simulators [25], they are still considerably slower than the alternatives.

If ontologies were religions, the constraint ontology would be agnosticism. No commitment is made to the types of objects in the world nor to the cause of change; all qualitative equations are written by hand. At one level, this is a liability since it makes the process of writing and debugging a system model much harder. However, by ignoring the complexity of qualitative modeling, researchers using the constraint ontology have illuminated the underlying mathematical nature of *every* approach to qualitative reasoning [37, 60].

The research reported in this book is based on Kuipers' QSIM formalism [38] — perhaps the best known example of the constraint ontology. This is not because I doubt the utility of the device and process approaches to modeling; I do not. But the mathematical elegance of Kuipers' definitions and the speed of the QSIM algorithm greatly facilitated the formalization, analysis, and implementation of comparative analysis techniques. Although we have not yet completed the implementation, we are currently working on integrating the DQ analysis algorithm with the QPE simulator for QP theory [21]. We expect no difficulties in this endeavor and are confident that both comparative analysis algorithms could be used with device ontology models as well.

1.3.3 Qualitative Simulation

Given a model of a system, many types of analysis are possible. The best studied form of reasoning is simulation — predicting the time varying behavior of a system. In the field of qualitative physics, this problem is called qualitative physics, but the same problem has been studied by other communities of researchers who call the problem TEMPORAL PROJECTION. While qualitative simulation and temporal projection have the same objective, to generate a description of the system's changing state over time, the representations used are quite different. Researchers studying temporal projection tend to represent change with modal logics (e.g., [57]) or probabilistic representations (e.g., [28, 29]) rather than the abstractions of continuous functions which are the signature of work in qualitative physics. Although some work has been done on integrating the different approaches [24, 46, 55, 63], more study is necessary to fully characterize the advantages and disadvantages of the three representations.

Qualitative physics researchers have developed three alternative approaches to qualitative simulation: envisionment, behavior generation, and history generation. The principle difference between the techniques lies in the representations that they produce to summarize behaviors over time. The first approach outputs a directed graph, called an ENVISIONMENT, in which vertices represent states, which specify the qualita-

1.3. Context

tive value for each parameter in the model, and edges represent possible transitions between qualitative states [8, 11, 21]. A BEHAVIOR is a path through the envisionment, i.e., a sequence of completely specified states denoting the system's change over time. While the envisionment graph is necessarily finite, infinite behaviors can result by following cycles in the envisionment. Thus an envisionment is a finite structure which captures all behavioral possibilities.

QSIM [38] exemplifies the BEHAVIOR GENERATION approach to qualitative simulation. Although the behavior-generation output is also a graph of completely specified qualitative states connected by arcs that represent transitions, this graph never contains cycles. Instead the output is a tree of states whose depth is potentially unbounded; every path from the root through the tree is a behavior. A disadvantage of this approach is the generation of a possibly infinite data structure, but an advantage is the ability to create an arbitrary number of new qualitative distinctions during the process of simulation. QSIM achieves this by creating new landmarks for a quantity when the quantity is between existing landmarks and its derivative becomes zero. For example, when simulating a ball being thrown up in the air, QSIM would introduce a new landmark representing the highest point of the trajectory. The introduction of landmarks is important for analyzing many physical systems, however at times too many landmarks are introduced and the resulting irrelevant distinctions choke the simulation process [40]. Because dynamic landmark creation can introduce an unbounded number of qualitative values and thus an unbounded number of qualitative states, it is unclear how to incorporate the technique into an envisioner.

One problem with both state-based representations is the need for the simulator to totally order all transitions in quantity values. For example, consider a system with two parameters A and B each with the initial value $(0, inf)$. In a state-based representation there is no clear way to state that both parameters will transition to 0 without specifying which transition happens first (or noting that they happen at the same time). When the simulator cannot determine the order, all three orderings must be considered. In the worst case the number of branching behaviors is exponential in the number of transitions. Besides this wasteful use of memory, the resulting structures contain irrelevant distinctions that confuse and complicate reasoning algorithms that manipulate behaviors. The HISTORY-GENERATION approach to qualitative simulation [72, 31] was invented to combat this problem. Instead of describing a behavior as a sequence of snapshot views of the system, histories slice through space-time in the orthogonal direction, following each object or parameter as it changes over time. By tracking changes in each parameter separately, and relating the times of transitions only when they directly interact, histories reduce the number of irrelevant distinctions and simplify reasoning. Histories also allow programs to reason about a larger class of systems, such as those with time-varying inputs.

Both of the comparative analysis techniques described in this book manipulate data structures representing behaviors. Since my techniques build on QSIM, I adopt the behavior generation approach to simulation. This assumption is not critical, however; both DQ analysis and exaggeration could be adapted to the other methods.

1.3.4 Types of Comparative Analysis

Earlier we defined the task of comparative analysis as the problem of determining how the behavior of a system will change if its structure is changed. But what kind of structural changes are admissible? This book is solely concerned with DIFFERENTIAL CHANGES (i.e., arbitrarily small increases or decreases) in the value of one or more parameters.

Another type of comparative analysis results from considering more drastic changes to the initial value of parameters. For example, what would happen to the behavior of a kitchen refrigerator if the compressor pumped refrigerant in the opposite direction (through the evaporator and the expansion valve into the condensor)? This question cannot be expressed as a differential change because in one case the refrigerant is moving with velocity V and in the other system the velocity is $-V$. Since for any interesting value of V the two flow rates are separated by the landmark value zero, the difference is non-differential. Although the techniques of DQ analysis and exaggeration are not directly applicable to non-differential comparative analysis problems, the topic is considered briefly in section 4.2 and an interesting example is presented in section 3.2.1.

A still more difficult version of the comparative analysis problem is called INTER-MODEL COMPARATIVE ANALYSIS [67]. This task is defined as predicting the difference in expected behavior resulting from a shift to a different model of the system. For example, suppose one was modeling a system of blocks, ropes and pulleys under the assumption that rope is inelastic. Inter-model comparative analysis could be used to predict what would happen to the expected behavior of the system if one carried out the analysis using a model in which rope could stretch. Would the blocks move faster or more slowly?

In general, inter-model comparative analysis is terribly difficult, however it is shown in [67] that in many real-world cases the problem can be reduced to ordinary differential comparative analysis and solved using the methods of DQ analysis and exaggeration that are described in this book.

1.4 Differential Qualitative Analysis

Differential qualitative (DQ) analysis is a powerful technique for solving comparative analysis problems. It predicts the effect of a small structural change by propagating the change through the equations modeling the system. The result is commonly called a "causal explanation" because it is viewed as a linear chain of consequences based on the original change or cause. For the technique to work, it is necessary to describe structural and behavioral perturbations in a formal language so that they can be manipulated symbolically. To this end, DQ analysis relies on relative change (RC) values using one or more perspectives (section 1.4.1). Once the original perturbation is described using RC values, a set of inference rules propagates the changes through the equations that model the system and produce a causal chain that embodies the explanation (figure 1.3).

1.4.1 Perspectives

Perspectives, the most important concept in DQ analysis, are best introduced with an example. Consider the horizontal, frictionless spring/block system shown above (figure 1.1). The system can be defined in Kuipers' QSIM [38] notation in terms of six parameters, each a function of time: spring constant K, mass M, position X, velocity V, acceleration A, and force F, related by Newton's second law ($F = MA$) and Hooke's law ($F = -KX$). Mass and spring constant are independent parameters that have constant values over time. The initial conditions are specified as follows: $M(0) > 0$, $K(0) < 0$, $V(0) = 0$, and $X(0) = x_0 < 0$.

This description may now be simulated, but because of ambiguities

16   Chapter 1. Introduction

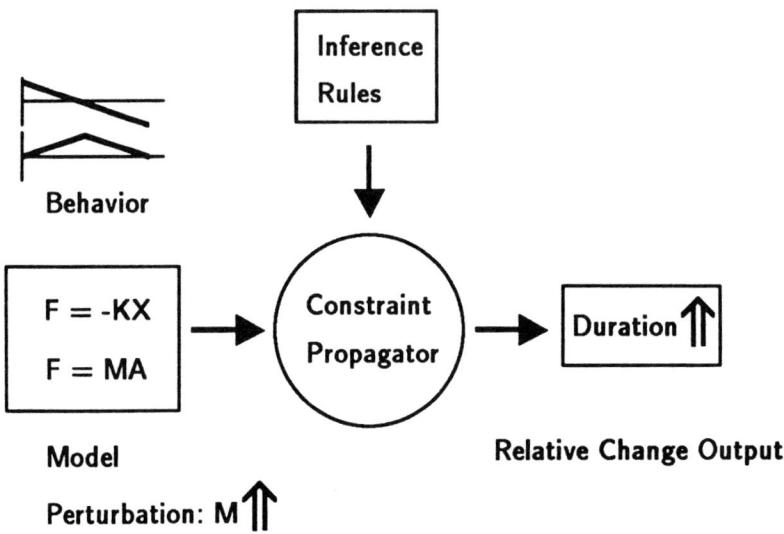

Figure 1.3
Overview of the DQ Analysis Algorithm

inherent in qualitative values [37], QSIM produces several possible behaviors for this system, including ones corresponding to increasing, decreasing, and stable oscillation. Although comparative analysis could be done on all of these behaviors, for this example, I assume the interpretation of stable oscillation (figure 1.4).

Now we are ready to pose a comparative analysis problem. "What happens to the period of oscillation if the mass of the block is increased?" The answer is that the length of the period increases:

> Since force is inversely proportional to position, the force on the block will remain the same when the mass is increased. But if the block is heavier, then it won't accelerate as fast. And if it doesn't accelerate as fast, then it will always be going slower and so will take longer to complete a full period (assuming it travels the same distance).

What kind of information is needed to produce this explanation? Take the first step: "The force on the block will remain the same." This is an example of a relative change (RC) statement since it expresses the

1.4. Differential Qualitative Analysis

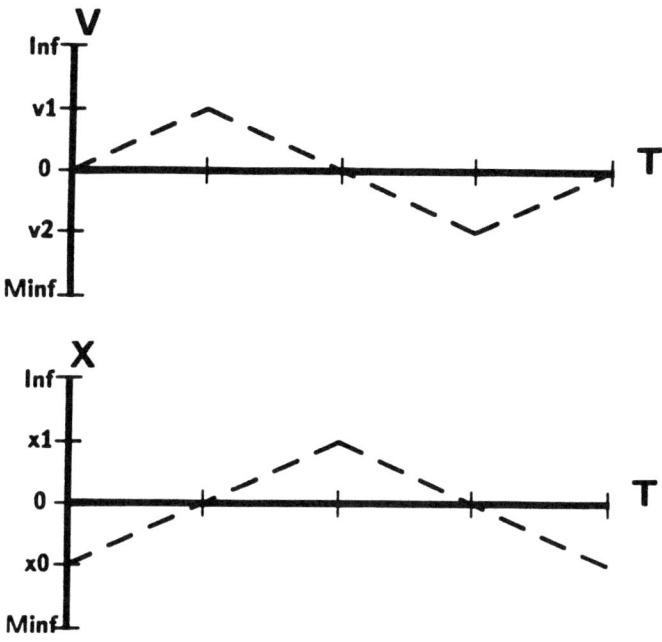

Figure 1.4
QSIM Behavior for Stable Spring Oscillation

relationship between values in the original and perturbed systems. To distinguish the perturbed force from the original, I denote it $\widehat{F}$ and plot it with dotted lines (figure 1.5). The question is what does it mean for force to be the 'same'?

Clearly, $F \neq \widehat{F}$ as a function of time. The corresponding values of F and $\widehat{F}$ are different for almost every possible time. The real meaning of "The force on the block will remain the same" is that F and $\widehat{F}$ are the same for all values of X. Although this reparametrization was not mentioned explicitly in the explanation, it is essential to the soundness of the argument.

In order to allow programs to generate and evaluate explanations like

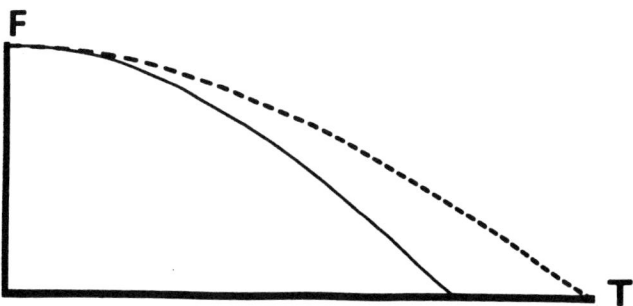

Figure 1.5
Actual Plot of Force versus Time

the one for the spring and block, it is necessary to take this implicit change of parameters and make it explicit. I do this with the use of perspectives. Thus the first line of the argument could be rewritten "If the mass is increased, force does not change from the perspective of position." Making perspectives explicit is the crucial step in performing DQ analysis to solve a comparative analysis problem. Once the notion of perspective is explicit, one can address questions like "Which perspective best suits a problem" and "What inferences are sound?" The answers are not as obvious as they might appear.

For example, consider the 'obvious' inference "Since it is going slower it will take longer to go the same distance." What does it mean for the block to be going slower? From what perspective is velocity lower? If velocity were lower from the perspective of time, then the conclusion would indeed be obvious. But just as with the force parameter (figure 1.5), there are times when the perturbed velocity is not lower than it was in the original system. Once again, position is the correct perspective. In fact, as shown in section 2.2, the explanation is correct, but it would not necessarily be correct if the perspective was a parameter other than position.

Reasoning about perspectives explicitly, and using sound rules of DQ analysis (section 2.2), the zetalisp program, CA, has generated the correct solution and an explanation like that shown above. In order to solve

1.4. Differential Qualitative Analysis

the question "What happens to the maximum velocity if the initial displacement is increased?" CA uses perspectives in a different way:

> Since K and M haven't changed, the force on the block is the same for any position that the block used to pass through. So the acceleration is the same for any position. But since the initial displacement has been increased, the block will already be moving when it reaches the old initial position, where previously the block was stopped. Since the accelerations are the same from here on, and the block is already moving faster, it will keep on moving faster and will have a higher maximum velocity.

The rules which generate this line of reasoning are explained in section 2.2.

1.4.2 Changes in Behavioral Topology

The previous section showed how the explicit use of perspectives could determine the relative change of parameter values and time durations given an initial perturbation. However, sometimes the perturbation results in change of a more fundamental nature. Consider the heat exchanger shown in 1.6. Hot oil flows through a pipe immersed in a vessel of cold water. A qualitative simulator such as QSIM takes this description and predicts the possible behaviors of the system as the oil cools while passing through the pipe. Figure 1.7 shows a possible QSIM behavior that corresponds to the case when the hot oil reaches thermal equilibrium just as it exits from the pipe. (Remember that since this is a qualitative plot, the apparent slope does not imply that these functions are linear.) Let's pose a comparative analysis problem. "What happens to the behavior of the heat exchanger if the thermal conductivity of the pipe wall is increased?"

The answer is that the oil will reach thermal equilibrium more quickly than before. And since the oil is flowing through the exchanger at the same rate, it must reach thermal equilibrium before leaving the pipe (figure 1.8). Thus, unlike the previous examples where the perturbation resulted only in continuous changes in various parameters, the perturbation of the heat exchanger causes a discontinuous change in the behavioral structure: the previously contemporaneous 'events' of thermal

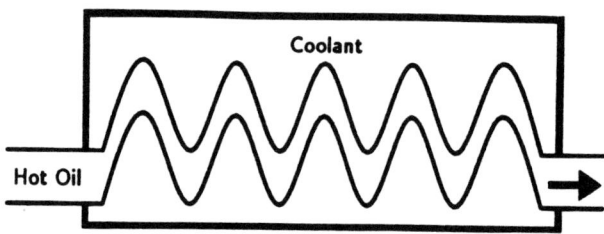

Figure 1.6
Hot Oil Flows Through Heat Exchanger

equilibrium and disgorgement from the pipe now happen at different times.

I call the switch from figure 1.7 to 1.8 a change in behavioral topology. This example is a simple case of topological change: the initial behavior was inconsistent and a single new behavior was indicated. However, the situation isn't always so easy. Section 2.5 describes how perturbations can lead to multiple consistent behaviors and presents heuristics for determining the most likely resulting behavior.

1.5 Exaggeration

Exaggeration solves comparative analysis problems in a completely different way from DQ analysis; it converts the comparative analysis question to a simulation problem concerning an exaggerated system where the original perturbation has been taken to a limit, and then analyzes the resulting behavior. This process decomposes naturally into three phases.

1.5.1 Transform, Simulate, and Scale Phases

Consider the heat exchanger from the last section (figure 1.6) in which hot oil cools as it passes through a cold water reservoir. Given the comparative analysis question "What happens to the oil output temperature if it moves through the pipe more quickly?" exaggeration uses the following reasoning:

1.5. Exaggeration

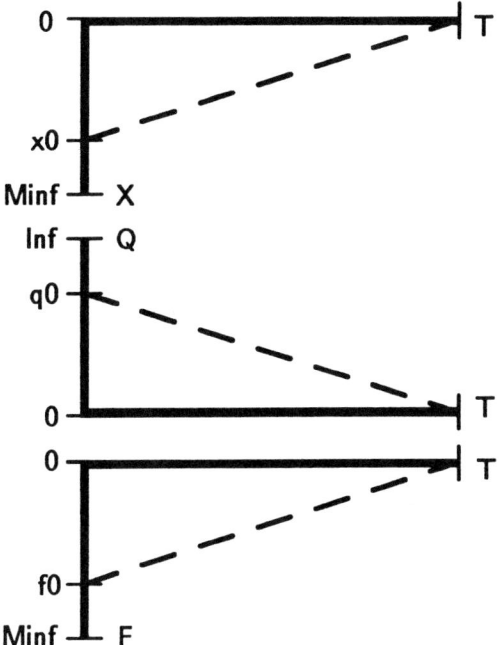

Figure 1.7
Initial Behavior of Heat Exchanger

If the velocity were infinite, then the oil would spend negligible time in the exchanger, so it would lose practically no heat. Thus increasing the speed even a small amount should cause the output temperature to rise.

This explanation clearly demonstrates the three phases of exaggeration (summarized in figure 1.9). The transform phase converts the comparative analysis problem to a simulation problem. Since the comparative analysis question concerned a perturbation in velocity, the transform phase generates a description of a heat exchanger in which the oil moved with infinite speed.

The simulate phase takes this exaggerated description and performs qualitative simulation to generate its behavior. In this example, the simulate phase predicts that the oil will exit after negligible time and after losing negligible heat. Although this phase is conceptually simple, many technical difficulties complicate the process of simulating systems with

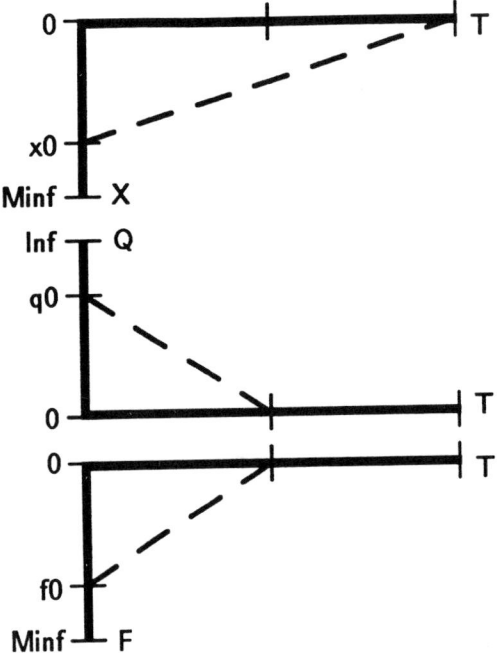

Figure 1.8
Perturbed Behavior of Heat Exchanger

infinite and infinitesimal parameters. As a result, the bulk of chapter 3 concerns exaggeration's simulate phase.

The scale phase takes the exaggerated behavior from the simulate phase and compares it to the original behavior in an attempt to answer the comparative analysis question. In this case it finds that the slow-moving oil lost more heat than oil moving at infinite speed. Since a large increase in velocity caused a drop in heat loss, the scale phase concludes that any increase in speed should result in an increase in exit temperature. Unfortunately, while the conclusion is correct for this example, the inference is not in general sound. It assumes (among other things) that the system responds monotonically to the perturbation. Unlike DQ analysis, exaggeration is not guaranteed to make correct predictions. On the other hand, exaggeration solves a wider class of problems than DQ analysis and often produces a more elegant explanation.

1.5. Exaggeration

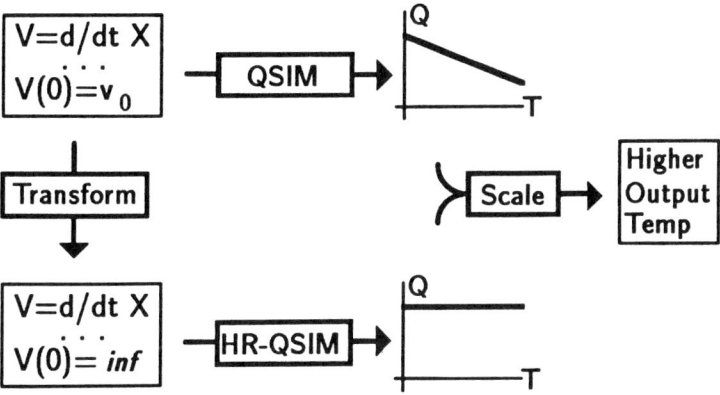

Figure 1.9
Overview of the Exaggeration Algorithm

1.5.2 Qualitative Hyperreal Representation

Since exaggeration works by transforming a perturbation to a limit and analyzing the resulting asymptotic behavior, it is critical to have a representation capable of describing infinitesimal and infinite values. I meet this requirement by extending Kuipers' QSIM quantity space notation using the hyperreal numbers of nonstandard analysis [49, 35].

The hyperreal numbers are a set of numbers (discovered in the early 1960s) that satisfy the real number axioms (e.g., associativity) but do not obey the Archimedian principle: "Every positive number, no matter how small, grows greater than one when added to itself enough times." In other words, the hyperreal numbers contain an infinitesimal element ϵ which is greater than zero, but remains less than one when multiplied by any finite natural number.[3] In fact, the hyperreals contain many such infinitesimals since the sum of two infinitesimals is a new infinitesimal (both the reals and hyperreals are constrained to a single additive identity, the number zero). Similarly, the hyperreals contain many infinite numbers — each one is the multiplicative inverse of an infinitesimal.

However, while there are many infinite hyperreal numbers, the *qualitative* hyperreal representation collapses them all onto the symbols *inf*

---

[3] Needless to say, this discovery stunned the mathematical world. See section 3.1 and appendix C for details.

and *minf* depending on sign. Every landmark value (e.g., q_0) has a halo of numbers that are infinitesimally close; the two halves of this halo are denoted (HALO q_0 +) and (HALO q_0 −) respectively. The positive infinitesimals, for example, are represented (HALO 0 +). Figure 1.10 shows some of the values in the hyperreal quantity space for the heat parameter.

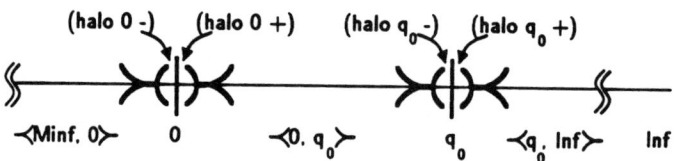

Figure 1.10
Some Values in the Heat Hyperreal Quantity Space

The qualitative hyperreal representation (section 3.1) of a parameter's state has two parts: value and derivative; square brackets are used to denote the qualitative state. Thus, to say that velocity is infinite at time t_0 and steady, one could write:

$[V(t_0)] = (inf, std)$

Since $V = \frac{d}{dt} X$, this implies that X is increasing infinitely fast at t_0; if its value is zero, one could write:

$[X(t_0)] = (0, (inc\ inf))$

To say that there is an interval of time, $\mathcal{A}$, when heat is infinitesimally less than its original value, q_0, and decreasing with infinitesimal (negligible) speed, one would write:

$[Q(\mathcal{A})] = ((\text{HALO}\ q_0\ -), (dec\ negl))$

To describe the interval, $\mathcal{B}$, when heat is between the landmark values of zero and q_0, not in the halo of either, and still slowly decreasing, one would write:

$[Q(\mathcal{B})] = (\prec 0, q_0 \succ, (dec\ negl))$

1.5. Exaggeration

The presence of infinite and infinitesimal derivatives necessitates an enhanced temporal representation. Elegance dictates that time should be treated no differently than other parameters, and a hyperreal abstraction indeed fits well. A qualitative state may last for a closed instant of time (written 0), or an open interval of infinitesimal (*negl*), finite (*fin*), or infinite (*inf*) duration. This raises a difficult problem for qualitative simulation — how can one tell how long it takes a parameter to change from one qualitative state to another? To solve this problem, the simulate phase of exaggeration uses two novel techniques: predecessor-persistence filtering and successor-arrival filtering.

1.5.3 Persistence and Arrival Filtering

The insight behind the dual techniques of predecessor-persistence filtering and successor-arrival filtering is the following observation about transitions in the qualitative hyperreal representation:

> It may take longer for a parameter to transition to a new qualitative state than it spends in its old state.

Lest this sound confusing, consider the following concrete example. Let I be a parameter defined as the identity function $I(t) = t$. Consider the length of the time interval, $\mathcal{A}$, in which $[I(\mathcal{A})] = ((halo\ 0\ +), (inc\ fin))$, defined as PERSISTENCE of the qualitative state in section 3.3.4. I claim that I persists in $(halo\ 0\ +)$ for *negl* time. For example, if I persisted in the halo for a standard real time, t_0, then that would imply that $t_0 \in (\text{HALO}\ 0+)$, in other words that t_0 is infinitesimal, not a standard real. Likewise 0 and *inf* persistences also lead to contradictions, thus I persists in $(\text{HALO}\ 0\ +)$ for *negl* time.

Now consider the time it takes for I to reach the next qualitative state, $\prec 0, inf\succ$ (formalized as SUCCESSOR-ARRIVAL TIME in section 3.3.5). I argue that I's successor-arrival time is *fin*. Suppose it takes *negl* time; then for some infinitesimal, t_1, $I(t_1)$ = a finite value. This is clearly a contradiction. In fact, all choices besides *fin* lead to contradictions as well.

And since only *negl* time passed reaching $(\text{HALO}\ 0\ +)$ from 0, I takes $fin - negl = fin$ time to arrive at its new qualitative state. In other words, even though there is no intervening hyperreal value sandwiched between $(\text{HALO}\ 0\ +)$ and $\prec 0, inf\succ$, I takes longer to reach its new qualitative state than it spends in its original state. The cause of this apparently mysterious behavior is the unintuitive nature of the order topology of the hyperreal numbers (explained in detail in section 3.3.2). Fortunately, the prescription is simple: a hyperreal qualitative simulator must distinguish between the time that a predecessor state persists and the time required to reach a successor state.

To see how these two metrics are used, consider the first few decisions the simulate phase must make concerning the infinite flow-rate heat exchanger. The transform phase constructs an initial state that has oil position equal to the left end of the pipe and increasing infinitely fast, $[X(0)] = (x_0, (inc\ inf))$. Heat is equal to some initial value and is decreasing at a finite rate, $[Q(0)] = (q_0, (dec\ fin))$. How long does this state last and what are its successors?

The notion of persistence, the maximum length of time a parameter can remain at a qualitative state, answers this question. To determine time one needs a measure of distance and speed. The speed measurement is easy; it comes from the parameter's the qualitative derivative. The appropriate distance measurement turns out to be the 'width' of the qualitative state, which is 0 for a point value. Since 0 divided by any nonzero rate is 0, and since both parameters have point values, they can persist in their current values for at most a point of time. This implies that in the successor state both position and heat have moved a negligible distance from their initial values: $[X(\mathcal{A}_1)] = ((\text{HALO}\ \ x_0\ +), (inc\ inf))$ and $[Q(\mathcal{A}_1)] = ((\text{HALO}\ \ q_0\ -), (dec\ fin))$. How long does this $\mathcal{A}_1$ last and what state succeeds it?

To answer this question, a simulator needs to reason about both persistence and arrival times. The width of each parameter's current values is negligible, $negl$. Since Q is moving with finite rate, its persistence is $\frac{negl}{fin} = negl$. Although velocity is infinite, X has the same persistence: $\frac{negl}{inf} = negl$. Thus persistence values show that the state will last for $negl$ time but do not predict whether X will change values before Q or whether they will transition at the same time. To determine this, arrival values are necessary.

The time required to reach one qualitative state from another is dependent on the distance between the two. Since both Q and X are moving from the infinitesimal halo surrounding a point value into an open interval of standard, finite real numbers, they must each traverse fin distance before arriving at their successor qualitative states. Like persistences, arrival times are computed by dividing distance by rate: Q arrives in $\frac{fin}{fin} = fin$ time while X only requires $\frac{fin}{inf} = negl$ time. This means that X must change qualitative states before Q, so the successor state has $[X(\mathcal{A}_2)] = (\prec x_0, inf\succ, (inc\ inf))$ and while Q remains in (HALO q_0 −).

Without the predecessor-persistence and successor-arrival filters, qualitative simulation using the qualitative hyperreal representation would produce a huge number of inconsistent behaviors. Such weakness in the simulate phase would render exaggeration unable to solve most comparative analysis problems. Efficient computation of persistence and arrival values, therefore, is central to exaggeration's success.

1.6 Conclusions

This work makes several contributions to the field of qualitative physics.

- It develops a precise formulation of relative change that extends earlier attempts [21] by explicitly accounting for multiple perspectives (sections 2.1.2 and 2.1.3).

- It presents inference rules for performing differential qualitative analysis and proves their soundness (section 2.2).

- It discusses an implementation of DQ analysis and uses it to test the theory (section 2.3).

- It extends the quantity space representation to account for infinitesimal and infinite hyperreal numbers (section 3.1).

- It discusses the implementation of a qualitative hyperreal simulator that uses many new ideas (four transition tables, predecessor-persistence filtering, successor-arrival filtering) to reduce ambiguity (section 3.3).

- It introduces exaggeration, a novel method for solving comparative analysis problems, and shows how qualitative hyperreal simulation is central to its operation (chapter 3).

- It compares the two comparative analytic techniques on a wide variety of dimensions so that future researchers can easily understand their strengths and weaknesses and use them effectively as black boxes.

DQ analysis and exaggeration solve comparative analysis problems in fundamentally different ways. DQ analysis uses inference rules that compute the sign of the partial derivative directly from a differential equation description, while exaggeration simulates both the original and an exaggerated set of equations and compares the resulting behaviors.

While neither technique is perfect, their strengths support each other. DQ analysis is sound: it produces no incorrect answers, but there are many cases where it doesn't answer at all. While exaggeration can produce a false predictions from systems that are not monotonic, it answers a wider class of problems than does DQ analysis. These complementary abilities suggest a powerful high level architecture. Given a problem, first try to solve it with DQ analysis. If that works, then a sound answer is guaranteed. If DQ analysis fails, then apply exaggeration. Now check exaggeration's predictions with all of the relative change values that DQ analysis is able to deduce. If they all agree, the chances are good that nonmonotonic behavior is absent. Finally, exaggerate the perturbation in the opposite direction and check that the resulting predictions are the opposite of the first transformation. Although there will still be pathological cases, these precautions maximize the heuristic power of the exaggeration method.

2 Differential Qualitative Analysis

Differential qualitative (DQ) analysis solves comparative analysis problems by propagating the effects of a perturbation through the structural model of the system. DQ analysis requires three inputs: a description of the system's behavior (from a qualitative simulator), the structural equations defining the system model, and a perturbation. A forward chaining constraint propagator uses a set of inference rules to deduce the system's resulting change in behavior. As these rules contain the knowledge necessary to perform DQ analysis, a discussion of them forms the bulk of this chapter.

However, before the inference rules can be explained, it is necessary to define more precisely how an input perturbation and the behavioral output can be represented as relative change (RC) values. This is done in section 2.1 which includes a recap of Kuiper's QSIM [38] notion of qualitative behavior as well as a formal definition of perspectives. Then in section 2.2, I present the inference rules which are a formal representation of common intuitions such as "When moving faster, less time will be needed to go the same distance." Section 2.3 describes the Zetalisp implementation. In section 2.4, I suggest ways of extending DQ analysis for use in a diagnosis system. Then in section 2.5, I discuss how toplogical changes (i.e., changes in the order that parameters transition to interesting values) can result from differential perturbations to a parameter. Although the bulk of this chapter assumes that this does not happen, this section describes how I relaxed this restriction. The result is a significant increase in generality for DQ analysis.

2.1 Preliminaries

As my formalism is based on that used by Kuipers for QSIM, I start out by summarizing his definitions.

Definition 1 *A* PARAMETER *is a reasonable function of time.*

See [38] for the actual definition of reasonable function; the intuition is that of continuity, continuous differentiability, and a finite number of critical points (places where its derivative is zero). Parameters are denoted by capital letters. Thus the velocity of a projectile might be described by the parameter, V, which is a function that maps time to velocity.

Definition 2 *Each parameter has an associated set of* LANDMARK VALUES *which is a subset of the range of the parameter. The landmark values always include (but aren't restricted to) zero, the values of the parameter at the beginning and ending times, and the values of the parameter at each of its critical points. A time, t, is a* DISTINGUISHED TIME POINT *of a parameter P if it is a boundary element of the set of times that $P(t) = p_i$ for some landmark value p_i.*

Landmark values are those values considered to be interesting to the human observer, and the times when these values are reached are of interest too. When a parameter becomes constant for an interval of time, then it will take on a landmark value for infinite number of time points. This is why the definition only considers the boundary times distinguished.

Definition 3 *A* SYSTEM *is a set of parameters that are related with a* STRUCTURAL DESCRIPTION *that consists of a finite set of qualitative differential equations defined using the following: time differentiation, addition, multiplication, and relation by monotonic functions.*

Kuipers' program, QSIM, takes a system and a set of initial values for each of the parameters and produces a set of possible behaviors for the system; the definitions below describe this behavioral output:

2.1.1 Qualitative Behavior

Definition 4 *Let $p_0 < \ldots < p_k$ be the landmark values of a parameter P. For any time t define the value of P at t as:*

$$\text{QVAL}(P,t) = \begin{cases} p_j & \text{if } P(t) = \text{landmark } p_j \\ (p_j, p_{j+1}) & \text{if } P(t) \in (p_j, p_{j+1}) \end{cases}$$

Define the direction of P at t as:

$$\text{QDIR}(P,t) = \begin{cases} \text{inc} & \text{if } \frac{d}{dt} P(t) > 0 \\ \text{std} & \text{if } \frac{d}{dt} P(t) = 0 \\ \text{dec} & \text{if } \frac{d}{dt} P(t) < 0 \end{cases}$$

Define, $\text{QS}(P,t)$, *the state of P at t, as the pair:* $(\text{QVAL}(P,t), \text{QDIR}(P,t))$

The qualitative state over the interval between two adjacent distinguished time points is defined similarly.

2.1. Preliminaries

Definition 5 *For any parameter P, the* BEHAVIOR *of P is a sequence of states of P:*

$$\text{QS}(P, t_0), \text{QS}(P, t_0, t_1), \text{QS}(P, t_1), \ldots, \text{QS}(P, t_{n-1}, t_n), \text{QS}(P, t_n)$$

alternating between states at distinguished time-points, and states on intervals between distinguished time-points.

Recall that a system contains a set of parameters each with its own landmarks and distinguished time points.

Definition 6 *The* DISTINGUISHED TIME-POINTS *of a system are the union of the distinguished time-points of the parameters. Thus the state of a system changes whenever the state of any parameter changes. The* BEHAVIOR *of a system is thus a sequence of system-states alternating between distinguished time-points and intervals.*

To perform comparative analysis it is necessary to abstract away from specific times, since two different systems may have analogous behaviors, but change states at different times. This is where my formal treatment diverges from that of Kuipers.

Definition 7 *A parameter is said to reach a* TRANSITION *when its qualitative value changes from one* QVAL *to another. A system is said to reach a* TRANSITION *when any parameter transitions. Transitions only occur at distinguished time-points, and every distinguished time point marks a transition. It will prove useful to be able to refer to these transitions independent of the time at which they occur, thus the sequence of transitions for a behavior will be denoted by the set* $\{\gamma_i\}$. *Every behavior also has a* TIME FUNCTION, $\mathcal{T}$, *which takes transitions to the distinguished time-points when they occur.*

The intuition is that each γ marks an event which changes the state of the system. When comparing two behaviors, I match them up event by event and use the time functions to tell whether one system is changing faster or slower than the other.

2.1.2 Comparing Two Behaviors

To compare two behaviors, they must be distinguishable; I use the hat accent to denote the second behavior. Thus $\widehat{\mathcal{T}}$ denotes the time function of the second system, and $\widehat{F}(\widehat{\mathcal{T}}(\gamma_1))$ denotes the second system's value of F at the time of the first transition. To simplify the problem of of comparative analysis, I start by only comparing systems with identical structural descriptions whose behaviors are topologically equal, as defined below.

Definition 8 *The behaviors of two systems, S and $\widehat{S}$, are* TOPOLOGICALLY EQUAL *if they have the same sequence of transitions, $\gamma_0, \ldots, \gamma_k$, and forall i such that $0 \leq i \leq k$,*

$$\text{QS}(S, \mathcal{T}(\gamma_i)) = \text{QS}(\widehat{S}, \widehat{\mathcal{T}}(\gamma_i))$$

and forall i such that $0 \leq i < k$,

$$\text{QS}(S, \mathcal{T}(\gamma_i), \mathcal{T}(\gamma_{i+1})) = \text{QS}(\widehat{S}, \widehat{\mathcal{T}}(\gamma_i), \widehat{\mathcal{T}}(\gamma_{i+1}))$$

The assumption of topological equality rules out possibilities like the block failing to make a complete oscillation if its mass was increased too much, but it does allow a certain pliability. If two behaviors are topologically equal, their respective sets of landmarks share the same ordinal relationships, but the underlying real values for the landmarks can be different.

Section 2.5 explains how this assumption can be relaxed, but even with it, the problem is nontrivial. Consider two oscillating spring-block systems. Even if the blocks have different mass and the spring constants differ, the two systems have topologically equal behavior. Yet the *relative* values of parameters such as period of oscillation may be different. These are the first changes that comparative analysis must determine.

Before I can explain the techniques for performing comparative analysis, I need to present a notation for describing the desired output. It's easy to compare the values of parameters at transition points:

Definition 9 *Given a parameter, F, and a transition γ_i, define the* RELATIVE CHANGE (RC) *of F at γ_i as follows:*

$$\begin{array}{ll} F\Uparrow_i & \textit{if } |\widehat{F}(\widehat{\mathcal{T}}(\gamma_i))| > |F(\mathcal{T}(\gamma_i))| \\ F\|_i & \textit{if } |\widehat{F}(\widehat{\mathcal{T}}(\gamma_i))| = |F(\mathcal{T}(\gamma_i))| \\ F\Downarrow_i & \textit{if } |\widehat{F}(\widehat{\mathcal{T}}(\gamma_i))| < |F(\mathcal{T}(\gamma_i))| \end{array}$$

2.1. Preliminaries

For example, if the two spring/block systems were both started with negative displacement and zero velocity (i.e., $X < 0$ and $V = 0$), their first transition would occur when X reached zero. This notation allows one to express that the second block is moving slower at the point of transition: $V\Downarrow_1$. It is important to distinguish the relative change notation from statements about values and derivatives. Even though $V\Downarrow_1$, QVAL$(V, \mathcal{T}(\gamma_1))$ is positive, and QDIR$(V, \mathcal{T}(\gamma_1))$ is *std*.

The curious reader may wonder at the use of absolute values in this definition. Relative change could also be defined by comparing signed values. I call the approach of definitions 9 and 11 MAGNITUDE SEMANTICS and the alternate approach SIGNED SEMANTICS. The two approaches are theoretically equivalent. However, since magnitude semantics appears somewhat more natural and simplifies various proofs, it is the default for the rest of the paper. In the places where signed semantics proves advantageous, it will be mentioned explicitly.

2.1.3 Comparing Two Behaviors over Intervals

It turns out to be somewhat more complicated to compare two behaviors over the intervals between transitions. What does it mean to says that one curve is lower than another over an interval? To do pointwise comparison, some notion of corresponding points is necessary.

The intuition for the requisite comparison is displayed in the explanation of spring behavior that was presented in section 1.4.1.

> If the mass of the block increases, the force on the block is the same....

Yet this doesn't mean force is invariant as a function of time—that isn't true. Consider the time when the small block is at its rest position; the spring applies no force. But since the large block is moving more slowly, it won't have reached the rest position and so there will be a force applied.

What the statement means is that force is invariant as a function of position. For every position that the block occupies, force is equal in the two systems, even though the two blocks occupy the positions at different times. Although parameters are defined as functions of time, they often need to be compared from the perspective of other parameters. Here it proved advantageous to consider force as a function of position.

Although people understand arguments that leave these changes of variable implicit, the notion must be made precise and explicit if computers are to perform comparative analysis. The notion of perspective is foundational.

Definition 10 *A parameter, X, is called a* COVERING PERSPECTIVE *over a transition interval (γ_i, γ_{i+1}) when the following three conditions hold:*

1. $\text{QDIR}(X, T(\gamma_i), T(\gamma_{i+1})) \neq std$
2. $X\|_i$
3. $X\|_{i+1}$

When just the first condition holds, X is called a PARTIAL PERSPECTIVE.

When a parameter, X, is a partial perspective, it is strictly monotonic so its inverse X^{-1} exists. This means that it is possible to reparameterize any other parameter, F, by composing it with the inverse:

$$F_X(x) = F(X^{-1}(x))$$

When X is a covering perspective, then F_X and $\widehat{F_X}$ have the same domain. Covering perspectives will prove especially important in the inference rules of section 2.2.

Definition 11 *Given a parameter F, a partial perspective X, and a transition interval (γ_i, γ_{i+1}), let F_X denote F as a function of X. Let U be the intersection of the domains of F_X and $\widehat{F_X}$*

$$U = (X(T(\gamma_i)), X(T(\gamma_{i+1}))) \cap (\widehat{X}(\widehat{T}(\gamma_i)), \widehat{X}(\widehat{T}(\gamma_{i+1})))$$

Define the RELATIVE CHANGE (RC) *of F over (γ_i, γ_{i+1}) from the* PERSPECTIVE *of X as follows:*

$F \Uparrow^X_{(i,i+1)} \quad if\ \forall x \in U\ |\widehat{F_X}(x)| > |F_X(x)|$
$F \|^X_{(i,i+1)} \quad if\ \forall x \in U\ |\widehat{F_X}(x)| = |F_X(x)|$
$F \Downarrow^X_{(i,i+1)} \quad if\ \forall x \in U\ |\widehat{F_X}(x)| < |F_X(x)|$

In other words, force is $\|$ from the perspective of position, if for all positions that are assumed in both simulations ($\forall x \in U$) the corresponding forces are equal. The definition of partial perspective says when is it possible to use a parameter as a perspective; section 2.2 addresses the question when is it useful to do so.

2.1.4 Time as a Perspective

Although comparisons of parameters that have been reparameterized by perspectives are more common, sometimes is is useful to compare via corresponding times. To keep notation consistent, I will call this 'using time as a perspective.' The goal is to come up with a meaningful definition for $P\Uparrow^{\mathcal{T}}_{(i,i+1)}$ and the other RC values.

One problem is that the duration of the two time intervals might be different. If so time acts as a partial perspective—one quantifies only over time in the shortest interval. Another problem is that the two transition intervals might start at different times; in fact one interval might end before the other starts, e.g., $\widehat{\mathcal{T}}(\gamma_i) > \mathcal{T}(\gamma_{i+1})$. The solution is to align the intervals before quantifying.

Definition 12 *Given a parameter P and an interval (γ_i, γ_{i+1}). Let $U = (0, d)$ where $d = MIN(\mathcal{T}(\gamma_{i+1}) - \mathcal{T}(\gamma_i), \widehat{\mathcal{T}}(\gamma_{i+1}) - \widehat{\mathcal{T}}(\gamma_i)))$. Define the* RELATIVE CHANGE *(RC) of P over (γ_i, γ_{i+1}) from the* PERSPECTIVE OF TIME *as follows:*

$$P\Uparrow^{\mathcal{T}}_{(i,i+1)} \quad \text{if } \forall t \in U \ |\widehat{P}(\widehat{\mathcal{T}}(\gamma_i) + t)| > |P(\mathcal{T}(\gamma_i) + t)|$$
$$P\|^{\mathcal{T}}_{(i,i+1)} \quad \text{if } \forall t \in U \ |\widehat{P}(\widehat{\mathcal{T}}(\gamma_i) + t)| = |P(\mathcal{T}(\gamma_i) + t)|$$
$$P\Downarrow^{\mathcal{T}}_{(i,i+1)} \quad \text{if } \forall t \in U \ |\widehat{P}(\widehat{\mathcal{T}}(\gamma_i) + t)| < |P(\mathcal{T}(\gamma_i) + t)|$$

2.2 DQ Inference Rules

This section presents a number of rules for computing and manipulating RC values, describes how the rules were incorporated into a computer program, and evaluates the program's performance.

- The duration rule formalizes "distance equals rate times time."

- The interval derivative rule expresses the relationship between one derivative and another, e.g., "more acceleration leads to higher velocity."

- The transition derivative rule predicts the final value of a derivative like velocity.

- The self reference rule says that every parameter appears unchanged from its own perspective.

- The perspective flipping rule allows a reasoner to change perspectives.

- The transition and interval constant rules show the relationship between constants and RC values.

- The end of time rule says that other things being equal a parameter changes more, the longer it is changing.

- The one's own derivative rule predicts what happens when a parameter is defined in terms of itself.

- The multiplication rule demonstrates that the familiar rules of qualitative arithmetic apply to RC values as well as derivatives.

Each of the rules are presented as theorems since they are proven sound. For simplicity, however, only the interesting and difficult proofs have been included in this paper. The rules have been implemented as part of CA, a ZETALISP program which solves comparative analysis problems using DQ analysis. CA uses a constraint propagator to derive implications of these rules. The resulting dependency structure can be translated into an English explanation[1] or used by an explanation based generalizer. Although CA is incomplete (there are some problems it for which it terminates without solving), it does answer and intuitively explain a large class of problems. Because the rules have been proven correct, CA is guaranteed to reach only sound conclusions.

2.2.1 Duration Rule

This rule is the basis for the very powerful inference: distance equals rate times duration. If the rate is slower in the second simulation, then it will take longer to go the same distance. Although this may seem obvious, perspectives are required to make precise the notion of 'rate is slower'; this makes it subtle. Before I can state the theorem, the notion of distance must be made clear.

---

[1] The CA implementation of DQ analysis has only a primitive natural language generator. Unless specified otherwise, all English text was produced by hand translation of computer generated dependency networks.

2.2. DQ Inference Rules

Definition 13 *Let X be a parameter which is increasing and positive (or decreasing and negative)[2] over the transition interval (γ_i, γ_{i+1}). Define DISTANCE-BY X over (γ_i, γ_{i+1}) as the relative change of the distance traveled by X over the interval as shown in the following table of qualitative subtraction:*

		Starting RC Value		
		⇑	‖	⇓
Ending	⇑	?	⇑	⇑
RC	‖	⇓	‖	⇑
Value	⇓	⇓	⇓	?

Note that the parameter X has a double purpose in this theorem: it has V as its time derivative, and it is also the perspective from which V is seen to ⇓. In the following, it may be helpful to think of V as velocity, and X as position.

Proposition 1 Duration Rule

Let V and X be parameters such that X is a partial perspective over (γ_i, γ_{i+1}). Given $V = \frac{d}{dt}X$, $V\Downarrow^X_{(i,i+1)}$, and $\neg$DISTANCE-BY$X\Downarrow_{(i,i+1)}$ then $\widehat{T}(\gamma_{i+1}) - \widehat{T}(\gamma_i) > T(\gamma_{i+1}) - T(\gamma_i)$, i.e. the duration of (γ_i, γ_{i+1}) will increase.

Proof: Note that the proof is not obvious: $V_X \neq \frac{dx}{dt}$. I prove the case in which DISTANCE-BY$X\|_{(i,i+1)}$. This is equivalent to requiring X to be a covering perspective. Let $a = X(T(\gamma_i))$ and $b = X(T(\gamma_{i+1}))$. Since X is a covering perspective, X has an inverse function taking position to time:

$$X^{-1} : (a,b) \to (T(\gamma_i), T(\gamma_{i+1}))$$

The function $\widehat{X}^{-1}$ also exists, has the same domain, and a possibly different range: $(\widehat{T}(\gamma_i), \widehat{T}(\gamma_{i+1}))$. By definition $V\Downarrow^X_{(i,i+1)}$ means:

$$|\widehat{V}(\widehat{X}^{-1}(x))| < |V(X^{-1}(x))| \quad \forall x \in (a,b)$$

Consider the case[3] where $V > 0$; this implies that all values of $\widehat{V}$ are greater than zero because otherwise the two systems would have different

---

[2] A similar definition is made for the cases of increasing/negative and decreasing/positive. This definition would be simpler to express in signed semantics.

[3] The case where $V < 0$ is similar; there is no case where $V = 0$ because then X would not reach a transition.

transitions, violating the topological equality assumption. This means that:

$$0 < \widehat{V}(\widehat{X}^{-1}(x)) < V(X^{-1}(x)) \quad \forall x \in (a,b)$$

So:

$$\frac{1}{\widehat{V}(\widehat{X}^{-1}(x))} > \frac{1}{V(X^{-1}(x))} > 0 \quad \forall x \in (a,b)$$

So:

$$\int_a^b \frac{1}{\widehat{V}(\widehat{X}^{-1}(x))} dx > \int_a^b \frac{1}{V(X^{-1}(x))} dx > 0$$

But by the chain rule, the time derivative of X^{-1} at x is $\frac{1}{V(X^{-1}(x))}$. So:

$$\widehat{X}^{-1}(b) - \widehat{X}^{-1}(a) > X^{-1}(b) - X^{-1}(a) > 0$$

Thus: $\widehat{T}(\gamma_{i+1}) - \widehat{T}(\gamma_i) > T(\gamma_{i+1}) - T(\gamma_i)$. In other words, the duration of the interval increases. □

It would be nice if one could show that the duration rule was sound if the premise was weakened to have $V\Downarrow_{(i,i+1)}^{P}$ for some arbitrary covering perspective P. However, the following proposition shows that this is false; just because $P\|_{(i,i+1)}^{X}$ for a perspective X doesn't mean that there doesn't exist some other perspective Z such that $P\Uparrow_{(i,i+1)}^{Z}$.

Proposition 2 Non–Uniqueness
Given a system with parameters P, X, Y, and Z such that X, Y and Z are covering perspectives over (γ_i, γ_{i+1}), then it is possible that $P\Uparrow_{(i,i+1)}^{X}$ and $P\|_{(i,i+1)}^{Y}$ and $P\Downarrow_{(i,i+1)}^{Z}$.

The example shown in figure 2.1 illustrates the proof by construction. The thin lines indicate the values of the first system while the dotted lines indicate the value of the second system. The first row shows that from the time perspective the behavior of P doesn't change. The second row shows the relative change of the perspectives. The third row depicts P_X, P_Y and P_Z.

Although this aspect of RC values may seem strange, it is actually inevitable. After all, everything is relative to one's perspective. Imagine a machine which hourly logs the linearly increasing concentration of alcohol in a fermentation tank. It produces the following sequence of

2.2. DQ Inference Rules

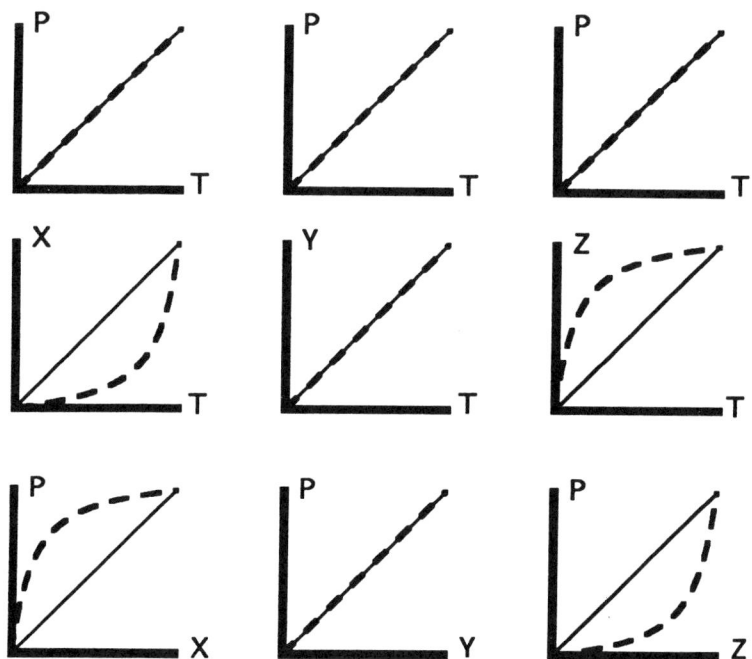

Figure 2.1
$P \Uparrow_{(0,1)}^{X} \; yetP\|_{(0,1)}^{Y} \; andP \Downarrow_{(0,1)}^{Z}$

measurements: 0.02, 0.04, 0.06, 0.08, etc. But in the identical tank nearby, the logging machine has a defective motor which runs too slowly and delays the measurements. Although the fermentation is proceeding at the same pace in both tanks, the second log will read: 0.03, 0.06, 0.09, 0.12, etc. Thus the plant inspector, who only sees the alcohol-time curve from the perspective of the logging device, might think that second tank was fermenting more quickly even though the only real change was a slowdown in the speed of the timing motor.

2.2.2 Derivative Rules

These rules connect parameters that are time derivatives. The first works over intervals and the second predicts RC values at interval endpoints. The intuition behind the first is: if a parameter is $\|$ at the start of an interval, but its derivative is $\Downarrow$ over the interval, then the parameter must be $\Downarrow$ over the interval. As always, the ubiquity of perspectives complicates the matter. Note the special role of X both as perspective and second integrand of A.

Proposition 3 Interval Derivative Rule
Let A, V, and X be parameters such that $A = \frac{d}{dt} V$, $V = \frac{d}{dt} X$, and X is a partial perspective over (γ_i, γ_{i+1}). Furthermore let A and V be positive over the interval (γ_i, γ_{i+1}). If $X\|_i$, $\neg V \Uparrow_i$, $A \Downarrow_i$, and $A \Downarrow^X_{(i,i+1)}$. Then $V \Downarrow^X_{(i,i+1)}$.

Proof: The chain rule makes this rule considerably harder to prove than the duration rule. It suffices to show that there exists some position such that $|\widehat{V}| < V$ for all positions up to and including this position. Once it is known that V goes down, the same argument can be used to show that it continues to go down. Thus it will stay down until γ_{i+1} is reached.

Let
$$\dot{\tau}(x) = \frac{dt}{dx} = \frac{1}{V(X^{-1}(x))}$$

Let
$$\ddot{\tau}(x) = \frac{d^2 t}{dx^2}$$

A can be expressed as a function of X
$$A(X^{-1}(x)) = \frac{-\ddot{\tau}(x)}{(\dot{\tau}(x))^3}$$

Because $X\|_i$, $X(T(\gamma_i)) = \widehat{X}(\widehat{T}(\gamma_i)) = a$. Since $A \Downarrow_i$ and $A \Downarrow^X_{(i,i+1)}$, it is the case that for all x in the half open interval $[a, b)$

$$\frac{\widehat{\ddot{\tau}}(x)}{(\widehat{\dot{\tau}}(x))^3} > \frac{\ddot{\tau}(x)}{(\dot{\tau}(x))^3} \tag{2.1}$$

Because $\neg V \Uparrow_i$ and since V is positive,
$$\widehat{\dot{\tau}}(a) \geq \dot{\tau}(a) \geq 0 \tag{2.2}$$

Substituting (2.2) in the denominator of (2.1) gives

2.2. DQ Inference Rules

$$\frac{\widehat{\ddot{\tau}}(a)}{(\widehat{\dot{\tau}}(a))^3} \geq \frac{\ddot{\tau}(a)}{(\dot{\tau}(a))^3} \geq \frac{\ddot{\tau}(a)}{(\widehat{\dot{\tau}}(a))^3}$$

So

$$\widehat{\ddot{\tau}}(a) > \ddot{\tau}(a) \tag{2.3}$$

And by continuity, equation (2.3) holds over a half open interval which may be written as $[a, c)$ for some c. This implies that the equation holds over the closed interval $[a, d]$ where $d = a + \frac{c-a}{2}$. But by the definition of $\ddot{\tau}$, for any $x_0 \in [a, d]$

$$\dot{\tau}(x_0) = \dot{\tau}(a) + \int_a^{x_0} \ddot{\tau}(x)\, dx$$

So for all $x \in (a, d]$

$$\widehat{\dot{\tau}}(x) > \dot{\tau}(x)$$

So for all $x \in (a, d]$

$$\frac{1}{\widehat{\dot{\tau}}(x)} < \frac{1}{\dot{\tau}(x)}$$

Thus by the definition of $\dot{\tau}$, for all $x \in (a, d]$

$$\widehat{V}(\widehat{X}^{-1}(x)) < V(X^{-1}(x))$$

So $V\Downarrow_{(i,i+1)}^{X}$ □

Above I pointed out the special role of X both as perspective and second integrand of A. It is natural to ask if the interval derivative rule is true for arbitrary perspectives. Unfortunately, it is not. Appendix B provides a counter-example which makes this point.

The interval derivative rule has an important corollary which predicts the value of the middle derivative, V, at the transition ending the interval. The intuition is twofold:

- If the object is accelerating slower, then its terminal velocity will be smaller.

- If the object accelerates for a shorter distance, then it will finish going slower.

Proposition 4 Transition Derivative Rules
Let A, V, and X be parameters such that $A = \frac{d}{dt}V$, $V = \frac{d}{dt}X$, X is a partial perspective over (γ_i, γ_{i+1}), and both A and V are positive over the interval. If one of the following conditions is true,

- $A\Downarrow_i$ and $A\Downarrow^X_{(i,i+1)}$) and $\neg V\Uparrow_i$ and DISTANCE-BY$X\|_{(i,i+1)}$
- $X\|_i$ and DISTANCE-BY$X\Downarrow_{(i,i+1)}$ and $\neg V\Uparrow_i$ and $A\|^X_{(i,i+1)}$

then $V\Downarrow_{i+1}$.

The rule is quite a mouthful, but that is simply because it is very general.

2.2.3 Perspective Rules

These rules deal with establishing RC values for perspectives and switching between them. The first is very simple, but turns out to be quite important. The intuition is that if the plant manager was foolish enough to try and use the logging devices to log their own speed, he wouldn't get a useful result. Both the normal and slow machines would record that they turned one full revolution during each revolution of the timing motor.

Proposition 5 Self-Reference Rule
For any parameter P, if P is a partial perspective over (γ_i, γ_{i+1}) then $P\|^P_{(i,i+1)}$.

The perspective flipping rules switches between perspectives. The intuition is that flipping perspectives (i.e., X^P to P^X) flips $\Uparrow$ to $\Downarrow$ if both parameters are positive and increasing over the interval.

Proposition 6 Perspective-Flipping Rule
If the parameters X and P are covering perspectives over (γ_i, γ_{i+1}), the sign of X equals the sign of P over the interval, and $X\Uparrow^P_{(i,i+1)}$, then:

$P\Uparrow^X_{(i,i+1)}$ if $QDIR(X, T(\gamma_i), T(\gamma_{i+1})) \neq QDIR(P, T(\gamma_i), T(\gamma_{i+1}))$
$P\Downarrow^X_{(i,i+1)}$ if $QDIR(X, T(\gamma_i), T(\gamma_{i+1})) = QDIR(P, T(\gamma_i), T(\gamma_{i+1}))$

If the sign of X is the opposite of the sign of P then the RC values are reversed.

2.2. DQ Inference Rules

Proof: I prove the case where both X and P are increasing; the other cases are almost identical. Let $a = X(\mathcal{T}(\gamma_i))$, and $b = X(\mathcal{T}(\gamma_{i+1}))$. For an arbitrary $x \in (a, b)$ $\exists p$ such that $X(P^{-1}(p)) = x$ because P is a covering perspective, and thus onto. Let $t_1 = \widehat{P}^{-1}(p)$, and let

$$\widehat{x} = \widehat{X}(t_1) = \widehat{X}(\widehat{P}^{-1}(p))$$

By the definition of $X\Uparrow_{(i,i+1)}^{P}$ it follows that $\widehat{x} > x$. Let $t_0 = \widehat{X}^{-1}(x)$. Since X is increasing $t_0 < t_1$. Again because P is onto, $\exists \widehat{p}$ such that $\widehat{P}^{-1}(\widehat{p}) = t_0$ so $\widehat{X}(\widehat{P}^{-1}(\widehat{p})) = x$. Now, $\widehat{p} < p$ because

$$\widehat{P}^{-1}(\widehat{p}) = t_0 < t_1 = \widehat{P}^{-1}(p)$$

and $\widehat{P}$ is increasing. But this means that

$$\widehat{P}(\widehat{X}^{-1}(x)) < P(X^{-1}(x))$$

and since x was arbitrary, it follows that $P\Downarrow_{(i,i+1)}^{X}$ □

2.2.4 Constants

Frequently a system will contain a few constant parameters whose values never change. The following rules are a simple way to express relationships between constants in the notation of comparative analysis. The intuition is that since perspectives just scale time, and constants don't change over time, all perspectives agree on the behavior of constants. If there was no fermentation happening in either vat (i.e. the alcohol concentration was constant in both vats), and the concentration of alcohol was higher in vat two, then both logging devices would agree on this even though their timing motors differed.

Proposition 7 Transition Constant Rule
If a parameter K is a constant over (γ_i, γ_{i+1}), and $K\Uparrow i$ then $K\Uparrow_{i+1}$.

Proposition 8 Interval Constant Rule
If a parameter K is a constant over (γ_i, γ_{i+1}), and $K\Uparrow_i$ then for all parameters P, if P is a partial perspective over the interval (γ_i, γ_{i+1}), then $K\Uparrow_{(i,i+1)}^{P}$.

2.2.5 Rules with Time as a Perspective

It is very common for one parameter to be the derivative of another with respect to time. When it is possible to reason about these relations from the perspective of time, greater power is achieved because the chain rule doesn't interfere as it does in the derivative rule. The only drawback is the fact that these rules are less frequently applicable.

The first rule says that if the a parameter is ∥ from the perspective of time, and the duration of the interval is increasing, then the parameter will have changed more by the end of the interval.

Proposition 9 The End of Time Rule
Let X be a parameter such that $X\|_i$ and $X\|^T_{(i,i+1)}$. Let s be the sign of X over the transition interval (γ_i, γ_{i+1}) and d be the sign of X's derivative. If the duration of (γ_i, γ_{i+1}) is $\Uparrow$, then

$X\|_i$ if $d = 0$, otherwise
$X\Uparrow_i$ if $s = d$
$X\Downarrow_i$ if $s \neq d$

The proof of this proposition is trivial and thus omitted, but it should be noted that it is easier to express using signed semantics. The second rule is used for determining a parameter RC value from the perspective of time. It applies whenever the time derivative of a parameter is a linear function of the parameter.

Proposition 10 One's Own Derivative Rule
Let X, V, and K be parameters such that $V = \frac{d}{dt} X$, $V = \text{MULT}(X, K)$, and K is a negative constant. If $V(\mathcal{T}(\gamma_i)) \neq 0$ and $\|_i$ and $K\Uparrow^T_{(i,i+1)}$ then $X\Downarrow^T_{(i,i+1)}$.

2.2.6 Rules from Qualitative Arithmetic

Research in qualitative simulation [11, 21, 69, 38] has developed constraints on derivative values for parameters in ADD, MULT, and monotonic function constraints. For example, if $X \times Y = Z$ and the derivatives of X and Y are positive, then Z must have positive derivative as well. These rules can be generalized to include RC values at transition points and over intervals. Here, I present just the rule for a MULT constraint at a transition point.

2.3. Implementation

Proposition 11 Multiplication Rule
If X, Y, and Z are parameters which are related by the constraint, $Z = $ MULT(X, Y), then the following table displays the possible RC values for Z at a transition point:

		Y		
		$\Uparrow_i$	$\|\|_i$	$\Downarrow_i$
X	$\Uparrow_i$	$\Uparrow_i$	$\Uparrow_i$	?
	$\|\|_i$	$\Uparrow_i$	$\|\|_i$	$\Downarrow_i$
	$\Downarrow_i$	?	$\Downarrow_i$	$\Downarrow_i$

The rule for the ADD constraint is similar, but complex to write using magnitude semantics.

2.3 Implementation

To test the theory of DQ analysis, a program called CA has been written on a Symbolics lisp machine. When a user selects an example, CA runs QSIM [38] on the example to produce a set of qualitative behaviors for the example. The user selects a behavior and also a set of initial RC perturbations. CA translates the QSIM behavior and perturbations into ARK[4] assertions. At this point ARK forward chains using the propositions described earlier in this section.

Each of these propositions is implemented as an ARK rule or more than one if the proposition used disjunction or negation. For example, the duration rule (proposition 1) is encoded as the three ARK rules of figure 2.2. The various definitions and propositions require about sixty ARK rules.

The simplicity of the transformation from proposition to ARK code provides confidence in the soundness of the implementation. And the fact that most rules get used in each explanation, establishes their utility.

Since ARK maintains justifications for all its assertions, it is possible to generate explanations for CA's conclusions. Consider the spring/block system. The question here is: "What happens to the period of spring oscillation if the mass of the block is increased?" The system is defined

---
[4] ARK is a descendant of AMORD [12] implemented by Howie Shrobe and others.

```
(⇒ (AND (D/DT ?x ?v)                              ; ?v is the derivative of ?x
        (DISTANCE-BY ?x (?start ?end) deq)        ; ?x travels the same distance
        (RC ?v (?start ?end) ?c (P- ?x))          ; the RC of ?v is ?c from
        (OPPOSITE-RC ?c ?oc))                     ;     the partial persp. of ?x
   (DURATION (?start ?end) ?oc)                   ; if ?c is ⇑, ?oc is ⇓
   duration-rule1)

(⇒ (AND (D/DT ?x ?v)
        (DISTANCE-BY ?x (?start ?end) ?oc)        ; if ?x travels ?oc distance
        (RC ?v (?start ?end) ?c (P- ?x))          ; and V's RC agrees
        (OPPOSITE-RC ?c ?oc))
   (DURATION (?start ?end) ?oc)                   ; then the duration is ?oc
   duration-rule2)

(⇒ (AND (D/DT ?x ?v)
        (DISTANCE-BY ?x (?start ?end) ?oc)        ; if ?x travels 'less' distance
        (RC ?v (?start ?end) deq (P- ?x)))        ; and V doesn't change
   (DURATION (?start ?end) ?oc)                   ; then the duration is 'less'
   duration-rule3)
```

Figure 2.2
Propositions Are Encoded Directly Into ARK Rules

in terms of six parameters: spring constant K, mass M, position X, velocity V, acceleration A, and force F obeying the following equations:

$$A = \tfrac{d}{dt} V$$
$$V = \tfrac{d}{dt} X$$
$$F = \text{MULT}(M, A)$$
$$F = \text{MULT}(K, X)$$
$$\tfrac{d}{dt} M = std$$
$$\tfrac{d}{dt} K = std$$

The initial conditions are specified as follows: $M(0) > 0$, $K(0) < 0$, $V(0) = 0$, and $X(0) = x_0 < 0$. Since energy conservation is not made explicit in the equations, QSIM produces several possible behaviors for this system. Although comparative analysis could be done on

2.3. Implementation

any of the behaviors, I assume in this example that the user selects the interpretation corresponding to stable oscillation.

Now the user selects the perturbation. Because some parameters depend on one another, not all parameters may be perturbed. The situation is analogous to the problem of specifying a unique solution to a differential equation where values must be given for the independent parameters and a set of boundary conditions provided. In this example, M and K are independent, while values for X and V are needed as boundary conditions. Thus to specify a comparative analysis problem, these four parameters need to be given initial RC values.[5] For this example, the perturbation consists of the following initial RC values: $M\Uparrow_0$, $K\|_0$, $V\|_0$, and $X\|_0$.

Given this input, CA correctly deduces that the block will take longer to reach the rest position ($X = 0$) from its original negative stretched position. Figure 2.3 shows the explanation that CA generates; this is created by throwing away all perspective information once computation is finished. I have annotated the explanation with the names of rules used in each step.

Since it is an initial prototype, CA makes no use of control rules. All possible forward chaining inferences are made using every possible perspective. Despite this, computation rarely exceeds a minute on any of the problems tested. If larger problems were to be attempted, some form of control would be desirable. Backward chaining from a goal pattern might increase efficiency. There appears to be no reason why the schemes of [14, 73] could not be applied. Possible heuristics include preferential investigation of certain perspectives and avoidance of certain computationally explosive rules like the perspective-flipping rule.

Another technique to speed up reasoning is explanation based generalization [41, 16]. Following the approach of [34], I implemented a postprocessing learning routine that takes CA explanations and produces new ARK rules which may be added to the ones presented above. While these new rules are independent of any particular domain (i.e., springs), they are optimized to solve a specific class of comparative anal-

---

[5]The choice of these four parameters is somewhat arbitrary. Mathematically, it would be equally reasonable to choose A instead of X, but this does not make physical sense; it seems intuitively impossible to directly affect acceleration. Since there is no way to deduce this from the differential equation model, it is essential for the person who constructs the model to annotate the structural description with the list of 'causally primitive' parameters — in this case, the four listed above.

Assuming M is increased:
    X doesn't change and   *(self-reference rule)*
    K doesn't change and   *(interval constant rule)*
    F equals K times X
    So F doesn't change.   *(multiplication rule)*
and
    M increases and   *(interval constant rule)*
    F equals M times A
    So A decreases.   *(multiplication rule)*
        So V decreases.   *(interval derivative rule)*
            So the time duration increases. *(duration rule)*

Figure 2.3
CA Generated Explanation for Increasing the Mass in the Spring/Block System

ysis problems. Less general than the rules presented above, the new rules are considerably more general than the specific explanation from which they are derived. Although I have completed the EBG implementation, the empirical evaluation of EBG's ability to increase DQ processing efficiency remains as an area for future research.

At present CA has been tested for multiple perturbations on over fifty comparative analysis problems using over twenty models (appendix F). While it always terminates and never produces an incorrect answer, CA doesn't necessarily deduce RC values for every parameter. Section 4 explains how this is a limitation of the DQ analysis technique independent of the CA implementation.

2.4 Extensions for Diagnosis

A natural application for comparative analysis is the automated diagnosis of continuous devices such as analog electronic circuits. Generate and test is a standard paradigm for hardware diagnosis [27]: candidate faults are proposed then evaluated to see if they account for the faulty measurements. Like all forms of comparative analysis, DQ analysis can be used to test any candidate faults that can be described as perturbations of continuous parameters in the device. In addition, however, DQ analysis has the potential to generate classes of candidate faults.

The key is to run the DQ inference rules in reverse. For example, the duration rule says:

Proposition 1 Duration Rule
Let V and X be parameters such that X is a partial perspective over (γ_i, γ_{i+1}). Given $V = \frac{d}{dt} X$, $V\Downarrow_{(i,i+1)}^{X}$, and $\neg\text{DISTANCE-BY}X\Downarrow_{(i,i+1)}$ then the duration of (γ_i, γ_{i+1}) will increase.

A natural question is "Can the duration rule be reversed? Is the converse sound?"

Conjecture 12 Converse Duration Rule
Let V and X be parameters. Given $V = \frac{d}{dt} X$ and $\neg\text{DISTANCE-BY}X\Downarrow_{(i,i+1)}$. If the duration of (γ_i, γ_{i+1}) $\Uparrow$, then $V\Downarrow_{(i,i+1)}^{X}$.

Unfortunately, the converse is false, as are the converses for other important rules such as the various derivative rules. The problem results from an implicit closed world assumption used in reversing the rule—that one of the three RC values, $\Uparrow$, $\Downarrow$, or $\|$, always applies. Proposition 21 shows that this is false.

Of course every transition interval could be broken into pieces such that a single RC value applies over each piece, but this misses the fundamental issue. The decomposition of time into transition intervals is forced by behavior of the system. Thus transition intervals have genuine qualitative importance. While sometimes useful, decomposing transition intervals into smaller pieces runs the risk of introducing irrelevant distinctions.

Although the converse of the duration rule is not sound, its converse might still be profitably used as a heuristic candidate generator. By reversing the DQ inference rules, it may be possible to provide focus to the search for probably faults in misbehaving analog circuitry.

2.5 Changes in Behavioral Topology

Recall that the inference rules of section 2.2 relied on the assumption that the perturbed behavior was topologically equal (definition 8) to the initial behavior. In other words, it was assumed that while the perturbation might change the relative values of parameters and stretch or shrink the length of time intervals, the underlying sequence of transitions would not change. Yet perturbations often will change the order or nature of transitions. This section explains how to recognize the changes and predict the resulting behavior. The overall architecture (figure 2.4) is an extension of the flowchart shown earlier (figure 1.3). The topology checker verifies the consistency of the predictions made by the constraint propagator. Since the inference rules are sound, any inconsistency must be caused by a violation of the topological equality assumption. A simple graph search technique locates the troublesome transition and determines the correct behavior.

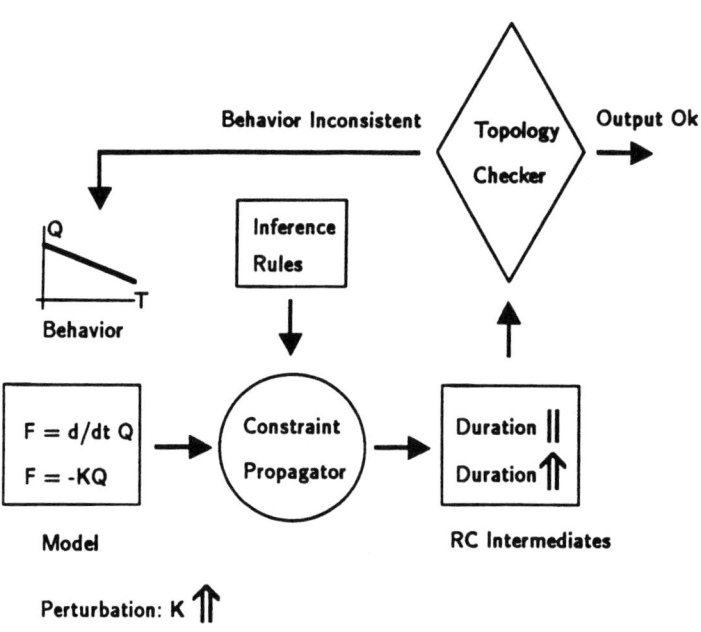

Figure 2.4
Overview of the DQ Analysis Algorithm

2.5. Changes in Behavioral Topology

To illustrate these computations, I use the simple example of the heat exchanger (figure 1.6) from section 1.4.2. This system is described in terms of five parameters, each a function of time: heat Q, heat flow F, thermal conductivity K, velocity of the liquid through the pipe V, and position of a unit volume of oil[6] X. The following equations are obeyed:[7]

$$V = \tfrac{d}{dt} X$$
$$F = \tfrac{d}{dt} Q$$
$$F = \text{MULT}(Q, K) \qquad (2.4)$$

In addition V and K are considered independent and assumed constant over time. The initial conditions specify the value for the independent parameters: $V(0) > 0$ and $K(0) < 0$, and also the boundary conditions: $X(0) = x_0 < 0$ and $Q(0) = q_0 > 0$. From this information the initial value of the dependent parameter, F, can be determined; denote $F(0) = f_0$. An invariant specifying that X must always be less than or equal to zero ends the simulation when the liquid individual leaves the pipe.

Given this description, QSIM (and other qualitative simulators [22]) produces the tree of qualitative states (STATE TREE) shown in figure 2.5. Since each path through the tree is a topologically distinct behavior, this tree represents three possible behaviors for the heat exchanger. The topmost path (QS1, QS2, QS3) corresponds to the behavior of figure 2.6 in which the system reaches thermal equilibrium just as the oil leaves the exchanger.

Because of its qualitative representations, QSIM cannot choose between the different behaviors for the heat exchanger; as far as QSIM is concerned, they are all plausible. Since DQ analysis works relative to a single behavior, one path through the tree must be chosen before running the rules of section 2.2. This selection of a behavior is a modeling decision; I assume that it is done by a human. The selection consists of a series of choices at each branch in the tree. By ruling out possible behaviors, each choice implicitly constrains the model of the system, restricting the possible real values associated with the qualitative values of each parameter. Thus the selection of behavior (QS1, QS2, QS3) makes

---

[6] For simplicity, the simplistic 'liquid-individual' model of fluids is used here; see [30] for a discussion of the problems with this model.
[7] For simplicity, this model does not distinguish between temperature and heat.

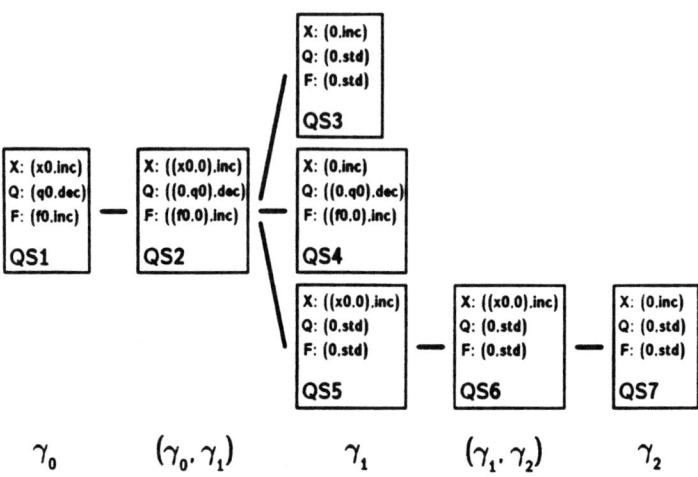

Figure 2.5
QSIM State Tree Generates Possible Behaviors

implicit assumptions about the relative values of fluid velocity, V, and thermal conductivity, K.

These implicit constraints are equivalent to the unambiguous selection of the initial behavior. However, the comparative analysis perturbation can weaken the balance of constraint in two ways:

- The initial behavior can be rendered inconsistent. Section 2.5.1 explains how the conflict is recognized and a new, consistent path is found.

- Alternate behaviors may become consistent. Section 2.5.2 explains how to locate other consistent paths through the state tree.

2.5.1 Initial Behavior Inconsistent

Suppose someone selected the path (QS1, QS2, QS3) as the heat exchanger's initial behavior (figure 2.6) and chose the perturbation $K\Uparrow$.

2.5. Changes in Behavioral Topology

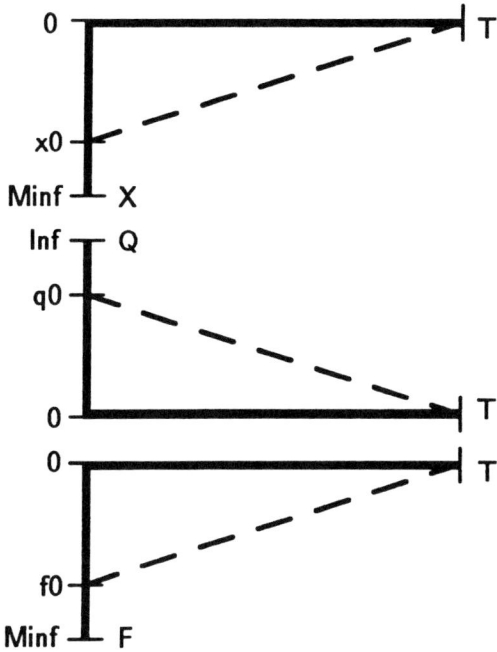

Figure 2.6
The Initial Behavior Corresponds to the Path (QS1, QS2, QS3)

The state QS3 dictates the two transitions, Q reaching zero and X reaching zero, in the same time instant. Since the perturbation causes heat to be lost more rapidly, QS3 can't be part of the final behavior. If one assumes that it is, the duration rule (section 2.2.1) deduces a contradiction, as follows.

When $K\Uparrow$, it follows that $F\Uparrow_{(0,1)}^{Q}$.[8] Thus the duration until the first transition is $\Downarrow$. However, being a constant V is unchanged by the perturbation, so $V\|_{(0,1)}^{X}$; the duration rule uses this fact to conclude that the duration $\|$. Hence the conflict. The perturbation causes heat to reach its transition quicker, but position is unaffected and will transition at the same time.

Behavioral inconsistencies are located by stepping through the transi-

---

[8] By the interval constant rule, the self reference rule and the multiplication rule.

tion intervals from earliest on, and checking the RC values for the interval's duration. Section 2.5.1 explains how to find all behaviors that avoid this single contradiction while obeying the initial constraints. Section 2.5.1 provides heuristics for eliminating inferior paths. Finally, section 2.5.1 shows how to check if the new behavior is globally consistent, not just a fix to the first contradiction. Note that all of these techniques depend on the DQ inference rules which are incomplete. As a result, while most inconsistencies are detected, it is not guaranteed that all inconsistencies can be found.

Finding Consistent Alternatives A simple observation about the inference rules of section 2.2 forms the foundation for the contradiction resolution method: only the duration rule can generate an RC value for a time duration. Therefore, the contradiction must be caused by two (or more) firings of the duration rule for the same interval. What distinguishes these firings are the different perspective parameters used in each application of the rule.

In the heat exchanger example, the two perspective parameters are Q and X. In the initial behavior, they reached transitions in the same state, QS3. But to achieve consistency with the perturbation, we must find a behavior where they reach transitions independently. This means finding a path which starts with QS1 and QS2, and passes through a sibling of QS3. The answer, of course, is the path (QS1, QS2, QS5, QS6, QS7) as shown in figure 2.7. This path illustrates the general case. A node representing the qualitative state at a time point (QS3) is replaced by three states: two at time points (QS5, QS7) and one for the interval connecting them (QS6). For the purpose of discussion, I shall call QS3 the FRAGMENTING POINT and the two time-point states which define our objective, the PREPOINT and POSTPOINT respectively.[9]

The problem, then, is to search the state tree among the siblings of the fragmenting point to find the pre- and postpoint states. We know that Q and X must reach transitions in different states, but which should reach its transition first? Consider the two duration RC values which

---

[9] Actually, this discussion assumes a simplified version of the general problem. I assume that the contradiction is caused by only two firings of the duration rule, and I assume that at the contradiction can be resolved by the addition of a single new transition. The general case is a straightforward extension. If the QS2 interval had three conflicting duration RC values, ⇓, ||, and ⇓, then QS3 could split into five states: three for time points and two connecting intervals. If multiple rule firings are allowed for each RC value, then correspondingly more paths are possible.

2.5. Changes in Behavioral Topology

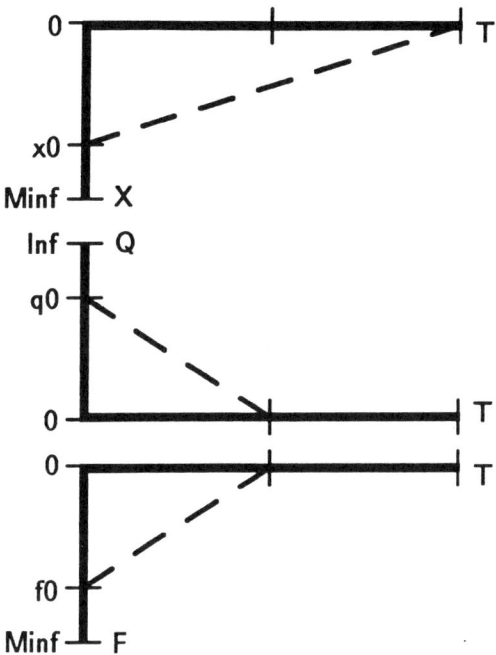

Figure 2.7
The Behavior Corresponding to the Path (QS1, QS2, QS5, QS6, QS7)

cause the contradiction. Since ⇓ specifies earlier termination than ∥, Q, the perspective parameter for the firing which produced the ⇓ value, will reach its transition first. This means that the prepoint will have $Q = 0$ and not $X = 0$. Since QS5 is the only state to meet this requirement, so QS5 is the prepoint. For the heat exchanger example, this state uniquely defines the new behavior, because only one path includes QS5; hence QS7 must be the postpoint. In a more complex example, however, there could be several candidates for prepoint and multiple behaviors passing through each one. The following conditions further restrict the possibilities.

- All parameters that reach transitions in the prepoint, must have reached transitions in the fragmenting point.

- All parameters that reach transitions in the postpoint, must have reached transitions in the fragmenting point.

- All parameters that reached transitions in the fragmenting point must reach transitions in either the prepoint or the postpoint, but not both.

While these conditions are loyal to the implicit constraints resulting from the initial selection of behavior, they are unfortunately not sufficient to guarantee a unique alternate behavior. The next section explains a heuristic that will guarantee a unique behavior but does not necessarily obey all implicit constraints.

A Heuristic For Eliminating Behaviors The conditions listed above produce a unique behavior except in cases where additional parameters besides Q and X reach transitions in the fragmenting point. When extra parameters reach transitions in the fragmenting point, one must choose where they should transition—in the prepoint or the postpoint. The following cases result:

- The parameter could be causally connected to either Q or X. In fact, this is the case with the heat exchanger: F transitions to zero in QS3. How did we know that F should reach its transition in the prepoint rather than the postpoint? We didn't even need to consider the question. By constructing the state tree, QSIM already handled the problem for use. It recognized that F must transition whenever Q transitioned; thus the state tree contains only this possibility. Since the topological consistency code searches the state tree, it automatically benefits from QSIM's work.

- There could be additional RC information about the parameter. For simplicity, this case was not discussed above, but suppose that the duration rule had fired three times with Q, X, and S as perspectives. If S and X both caused the duration rule to deduce an RC value of $\|$, then both X and S should reach transitions in the postpoint. Unfortunately, other RC values complicate the analysis. If three different RC values result from the three firings, then the fragmenting point will split into five states. The details are messy, but the concepts for resolution are similar to those described above.

2.5. Changes in Behavioral Topology

- The parameter could be independent of the perturbation without the inference rules deducing this. As with the previous case (where the independence, duration ||, *was* deduced) the parameter should transition in whichever state has duration ||.

- The perturbation could change the parameter's transition time without the inference rules deducing this. The correct behavior is not predictable since the change in duration is not known.

Since there is no way to correctly handle the last case, a reasonable heuristic is to assume that it never happens. This corresponds to Occam's Razor. Assume that unless the duration rule says otherwise, the perturbation does not change the transition time of any parameters. Thus if the heat exchanger example had an extra parameter, S, which reached a transition in QS3, then we should assume that S transitions with X in QS7.

Ensuring Global Consistency Using the heuristics, the algorithm described above is guaranteed to find a unique postpoint. But there may be several state tree paths that pass through this post point. To locate a single new behavior, the program must step through the original behavior from the fragmenting point onwards. Every time a branch in the tree is taken, the corresponding descendant of the postpoint should be selected as well. When the original behavior reaches a leaf, a unique new behavior will result. Unfortunately, there are two reasons why processing must continue.

- Many RC values must be recomputed. Because the RC values refer to transition points and intervals, all values from the fragmenting interval onward will be incorrect. This isn't very surprising; after all, we started with conflicting duration RC values in the first place. Given the new behavior, the inference rules of section 2.2 must be rerun to generate a consistent set of RC values.

- What if these rules generate a new contradiction? There is no guarantee that the new behavior is topologically sound. However, if conflicting duration RC values *are* generated for an interval, that interval must occur after any interval which caused a previous conflict. Thus each cycle of inference rules and topology resolution guarantees that the time of first inconsistency increases. Since all behaviors are finite, the cycle must eventually terminate.

It is possible that a more sophisticated algorithm could eliminate this cyclic approach by a detailed analysis of the initial behavior. Since all parameters are continuous functions of time, no (small) perturbation can invalidate the initial behavior unless the behavior has a state in which two parameters transition. Perhaps all such states could be checked at once.

2.5.2 Finding Other Consistent Behaviors

Sometimes a perturbation will be consistent with the initial behavior, i.e. not violate the implicit constraints, but will weaken them instead. In other words, there may be several behaviors which are consistent with the perturbed initial behavior. Since the QSIM state tree records the results of past transition analysis, a simple search technique suffices to find the behaviors that are consistent with both the perturbation and the implicit constraints. Four cases need to be checked: compacting, stalling, kick-starting, and splitting.

- COMPACTING

    When the duration of an interval is decreasing, perhaps the states on either side will merge into a single transition. Suppose the initial behavior is the path (QS1, QS2, QS5, QS6, QS7) as shown in 2.7, and suppose the perturbation is $K\Downarrow$. Although the initial behavior is consistent with this perturbation, it is possible that thermal equilibrium will be delayed until the precise moment that the oil leaves the pipe. This would correspond to the behavior (QS1, QS2, QS3) as shown in figure 2.6. Whenever the duration of an interval (e.g., QS6) is getting shorter, CA looks for an uncle state which has the same transitions (i.e. the same parameters reaching the same landmarks) as the union of the parent and child of the interval state. Q and F reach transitions in QS5, the parent of QS6, and X transitions in the child of QS6. So the search produces the uncle, QS3, and constructs the corresponding path through it.

2.5. Changes in Behavioral Topology

- STALLING

  If the duration of an interval is ⇑, then maybe the parameters will not transition in finite time. CA suggests a behavior consisting of the path which ends at the interval state.

- KICK-STARTING

  Kick starting is the inverse of stalling. If the initial behavior ended with a terminal interval, and the perturbation is causing the interval's duration to ⇓, then maybe some parameter will transition in finite time. CA returns all paths that pass through the interval state.

- SPLITTING

  Splitting happens when the duration rule[10] deduces a single RC value of ⇑ or ⇓ from two different perspectives. For example, consider the heat exchange with an initial behavior of (QS1, QS2, QS3) and the perturbation of K⇑ and V⇑. Since thermal conductivity is higher, equilibrium will occur sooner, but since the oil is moving faster, it will get out quicker. Both parameters lead the duration rule to conclude QS3 will occur quicker; thus the initial behavior is consistent. But so is every behavior. If the thermal conductivity is much higher and velocity is only a little higher, then the behavior (QS1, QS2, QS5, QS6, QS7) will result. If V was increased more than K then the path (QS1, QS2, QS4) would result. Because the perturbation was specified in qualitative terms, there isn't enough information to resolve the ambiguity and CA must return all possible splits of the two parameters Q and X.

Like the techniques of section 2.5.1, my methods for finding other consistent behaviors are dependent on the DQ inference rules. As a result they are neither complete nor sound. For example, suppose the duration of an interval was ⇓, but the duration rule had not deduced this fact. Then compaction would not be considered and a possibly consistent behavior would not be considered. Similarly, one of the techniques could suggest a behavior which appears consistent only because the DQ rules were inadequate to expose a contradiction.

---

[10]Splitting is the only case that analyzes justifications and depends on the fact that the duration rule is the only way to generate a duration RC value. Compacting, stalling, and kick-starting only require the RC value and access to the state tree.

2.6 Summary

Differential qualitative (DQ) analysis takes three inputs: a qualitative behavior as produced by QSIM, the underlying qualitative structural equations that produced the behavior, and a perturbation as specified by initial relative change values for the exogenous parameters. Given these inputs, DQ analysis uses a set of inference rules to propagate the effects of the perturbation through the structural model. Because the inference rules are proven mathematically sound, DQ analysis can not generate an incorrect answer or explanation to a comparative analysis question. However, as explained in chapter 4, DQ analysis is incomplete — it can not answer every comparative analysis question. However, it does answer many questions, and the simple causal nature of the explanations produced make it a powerful and useful techinque.

3 Exaggeration

Exaggeration's approach to comparative analysis is very different from that of DQ analysis. Instead of tracing the effect of a perturbation through the causal structure of the system, exaggeration considers the behavior of a system in which the perturbation is taken to a limiting value. If this new system has *qualitatively different* behavior than the original, then exaggeration postulates a general trend caused by the perturbation. For example, consider the heat exchanger example of section 2.5 and the comparative analysis question 'What would happen to the output temperature of the oil if it moved faster through the pipe?' Exaggeration produces the following answer:

> If the oil moved infinitely fast, it would spend almost no time in the exchanger. Since almost no heat would be lost, the oil would exit very hot. Thus increasing the fluid flow rate a small amount should increase the output temperature a bit as well.

Thus exaggeration changes a comparative analysis question into a simulation problem about a system with infinite or infinitesimal valued parameters. Figure 3.1 provides an overview of the program, EXAG, that implements the theory of exaggeration in three phases. The TRANSFORM PHASE takes a structural description of the system and a perturbation and produces a new model using the qualitative hyperreal representation (section 3.1.2). The SIMULATE PHASE (denoted HR-QSIM in the figure) simulates this hyperreal model to produce an exaggerated behavior that is qualitatively different from the behavior QSIM produces using the original model: in one case the heat has dropped a finite amount while in the other it has dropped only a negligible amount. Finally, the SCALE PHASE compares the two behaviors and predicts the answer to the original comparative analysis question.

Since exaggeration is critically dependent on the notions of infinite and infinitesimal values, the next section defines a qualitative representation based on the hyperreal numbers. The remainder of this chapter discusses the transform, simulate, and scale phases in turn. Then, in chapter 4, I compare the strengths and weaknesses of exaggeration and DQ analysis.

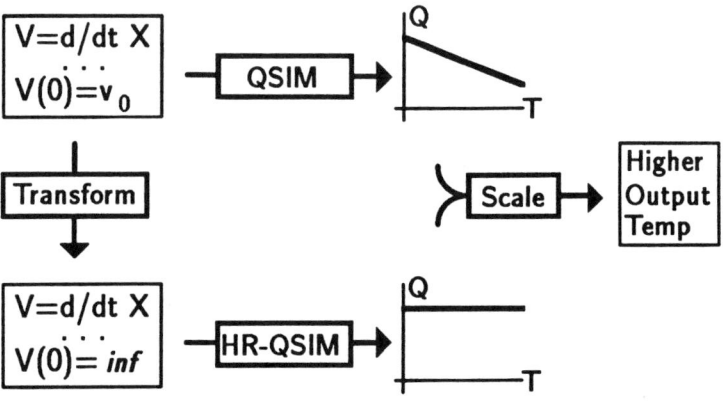

Figure 3.1
Overview of the Exaggeration Algorithm

3.1 Qualitative Representation Extensions

Various AI researchers have attempted to incorporate into their programs the seemingly intuitive notion of infinite and infinitesimal numbers. Frequently, the result has been inconsistent. To avoid this fate, I base the theory of exaggeration on the sound mathematical formulations of nonstandard analysis [49].

3.1.1 The Hyperreal Numbers

Although the technical details behind nonstandard analysis are tricky, the intuition is simple. This section sketches an outline of the subject, simplified from Davis and Hersh's Scientific American article [5]. For a discussion of more detailed sources, see appendix C.

Many mathematicians, including Newton and Leibniz, have used the concept of an infinitesimal when reasoning about geometry, but only as an informal aid. Everyone recognized that the very idea of an infinitesimal is self-contradictory since it violates the Archimedian principle: "Every positive number, no matter how small, grows greater than one when added to itself enough times." Thus while infinitesimals might be a useful tool on the route to a theorem, any final, rigorous proof must avoid them, perhaps using the concept of limit instead.

3.1. Qualitative Representation Extensions

This all changed in the early 1960s when Abraham Robinson proved the existence of infinitesimals having the same 'properties' as ordinary real numbers. The trick was defining 'properties' correctly so that the Archimedian principle did not count as a property. He defined property to mean "expressible in first order predicate calculus." For example, one can use this language to express the property of having an inverse as follows:

$$\forall x \ (x = 0) \vee (\exists y \ xy = 1)$$

Robinson's proof starts with the finite, real numbers; call them the STANDARD REALS. Let K_0 be the set of all first order predicate calculus sentences which are true about the standard reals. Of course, K_0 is such a big set that there is no way to know its contents (short of proving every possible calculus theorem), but by definition the standard reals are a model of K_0. It turns out, however, that there are other models of K_0 besides the standard reals, and one of these models contains infinitesimals. The proof is simple given a result called the compactness theorem [19] which states: "A set of sentences, K, has a model if every finite subset of K has a model."

From this result, the existence of infinitesimals follows trivially! Consider the following infinite subset of K_0, where I denotes an arbitrary constant (not a free variable).

$$0 < I < \frac{1}{2}$$

$$0 < I < \frac{1}{3}$$

. . .

And so on... Every finite subset of these sentences will be true of the real numbers, since a finite subset will contain a smallest fraction, $\frac{1}{N}$, and so an interpretation that assigns I the value $\frac{1}{N+1}$ will satisfy those sentences. Thus the compactness theorem says that there is a model that contains a positive number, I, which is less than $\frac{1}{M}$ for every M, in other words an infinitesimal! This model is often called NONSTANDARD simply because it is different from the standard reals;

however, to distinguish the model satisfying this set of sentences from other nonstandard models, I use the name HYPERREALS.

Since the hyperreals are a model for K_0, they act much like the standard real numbers. For example, they are closed under addition and multiplication. In fact, the hyperreals can be thought of as a superset (technically, 'field extension') of the standard reals. The product of a standard real and an infinitesimal is an infinitesimal. The product of two infinitesimals is a new infinitesimal. Thus it turns out that there are (uncountably) many infinitesimals. Since K_0 includes the fact that nonzero standard real numbers have multiplicative inverses, nonzero hyperreals must also. The inverse of an infinitesimal is called an infinite number; there are many of these also. The sum of a standard real and an infinitesimal is not a standard real, it is a hyperreal number that is infinitesimally close to the standard real. Since all infinitesimal numbers could be added to the same standard real, it follows that every standard real number has a HALO of hyperreal numbers surrounding it, at negligible distance, isolating it from other standard reals. The infinitesimals are simply the halo of zero.

One more fact proves very important. Just as there is no smallest or largest positive, standard real number, there is no largest infinitesimal and no smallest infinity. This fact occupies considerable attention in the discussion of the simulate phase (section 3.3).

3.1.2 The Qualitative Hyperreals

While the QSIM qualitative representation [38] is an elegant abstraction of the standard real numbers, it does not suffice for the hyperreals. Like Kuipers, I consider parameters to be functions from time to their respective domains (positions, heats, etc.), but they are now functions to and from the hyperreal numbers. Kuipers' restriction that each parameter be a REASONABLE FUNCTION, is still valid; the intuition is that they are continuous, continuously differentiable, and have at most finitely many critical points in any bounded interval [38].

It is still useful to decompose the state of a parameter into two parts: qualitative value and qualitative direction, but each of these parts must be extended. In the QSIM representation, the value part is either an interesting LANDMARK VALUE such as 0 or q_0 or the open interval between two landmark values, e.g., the interval $(0, \mathit{inf})$. Since landmark values are a major way of introducing meaningful qualitative distinctions into a

3.1. Qualitative Representation Extensions

domain model, they are kept in the qualitative hyperreal representation. However, *inf* and *minf* are no longer considered landmark values; they are treated specially.

Definition 14 *Let $p_0 < \ldots < p_k$ be the landmark values of a parameter P. For any time t define the qualitative hyperreal value of P at t as:*

$$\text{HR-QVAL}(P(t)) = \begin{cases} \inf & \text{if } P(t) > \text{every finite number} \\ \minf & \text{if } P(t) < \text{every finite number} \\ p_j & \text{if } P(t) = \text{landmark } p_j \\ (\text{HALO } p_j \;+) & \text{if } P(t) - p_j \text{ is infinitesimal} > 0 \\ (\text{HALO } p_j \;-) & \text{if } P(t) - p_j \text{ is infinitesimal} < 0 \\ \prec p_j, p_{j+1} \succ & \text{if } P(t) - p_j \text{ and } p_{j+1} - P(t) \text{ are} \\ & \text{both non-infinitesimal and} > 0 \\ \prec p_k, \inf \succ & \text{if } P(t) \text{ is finite and } P(t) - p_k \text{ is} \\ & \text{non-infinitesimal} > 0 \\ \prec \minf, p_0 \succ & \text{if } P(t) \text{ is finite and } P(t) - p_0 \text{ is} \\ & \text{non-infinitesimal} < 0 \end{cases}$$

If the same HR-QVAL *describes a parameter for all instants in an interval of time, $\mathcal{A}$, then one may write* HR-QVAL$(P(\mathcal{A}))$.

Thus all positive infinities are collapsed onto the symbol *inf* and all negative infinite numbers are denoted *minf*. Every finite landmark, p, has an infinitesimal halo above and below it; these halos are denoted (HALO $p\;+$) and (HALO $p\;-$) respectively. The positive infinitesimals, for example, are represented (HALO $0\;+$). The QSIM expression for an open interval, (p_1, p_2), is not used since it overlaps with (HALO $p_1\;+$) and (HALO $p_2\;-$). The definition of $\prec p_1, p_2 \succ$ is equivalent to the difference between the interval (p_1, p_2) and the two halos.

It also proves useful to extend the representation for qualitative direction. In the QSIM representation the derivative part of a qualitative state is a simple description of the sign of the parameter's derivative: *inc*, *dec*, or *std*. The qualitative hyperreal representation distinguishes between increasing parameters depending on how fast they are growing.

Definition 15 *Let P be a parameter and t be a time. Define the qualitative hyperreal direction of P at t as the pair of its qualitative direction and its derivative's order of magnitude:*

$$\text{HR-QDIR}(P(t)) = (\text{QDIR}(P(t)) \; \text{OM}(\tfrac{d}{dt} P(t)))$$

The qualitative direction, QDIR, is either inc, dec, or std corresponding to increasing, decreasing, or zero (steady) time derivative [38]. Define order of magnitude as:

$$\text{OM}(x) = \begin{cases} \inf & \text{if } |x| > \text{every finite number} \\ \text{fin} & \text{if } |x| = \text{a positive standard real number} \\ \text{negl} & \text{if } |x| = \text{negligible, i.e. a positive infinitesimal} \\ 0 & \text{if } x = 0 \end{cases}$$

If the same HR-QDIR describes a parameter for all instants in an interval of time, $\mathcal{A}$, then one may write HR-QDIR$(P(\mathcal{A}))$.

Thus (dec inf) denotes the HR-QDIR of a parameter that is decreasing infinitely fast. If a parameter's HR-QDIR is (std 0), then it may be abbreviated std since 0 is the only possible order of magnitude of std.

Definition 16 *Define the hyperreal qualitative representation, HR-QR, of a parameter P at the time t (or the interval of time, $\mathcal{A}$) as the pair of its qualitative hyperreal value and direction:*

$$[P(t))] \equiv (\text{HR-QVAL}(P(t)), \text{HR-QDIR}(P(t)))$$

The HR-QR of a parameter is denoted by square brackets. The qualitative hyperreal STATE *of a system at a time point or interval is the set of HR-QRs for all the parameters in the system.*

3.1.3 Behaviors over Hyperreal Time

Definition 17 *A parameter P is said to* TRANSITION *whenever it changes to a new qualitative value.*

These transitions are similar to, but less intuitive than changes between QSIM qualitative values. For example, QSIM transitions always happen at a well defined point of time (called a 'distinguished time point' by Kuipers [38]). This is no longer true in the qualitative hyperreal representation. When a parameter changes from the value (halo 0 +) to ≺0, inf≻, for example, there is no single time point when the transition happens. This is discussed more in section 3.3.2.

Like the standard QSIM equivalent, a HYPERREAL BEHAVIOR is defined as a sequence of qualitative states. However, the temporal nature of these sequences is not as simple as it is in the QSIM case where a state representing a time point is always succeeded by a state over an open time interval. As explained more fully in the sections on predecessor-persistence (3.3.4) and successor-arrival filtering (3.3.5), qualitative hyperreal states can persist for a closed point of time (written 0) or open intervals of infinite (*inf*), finite (*fin*), or negligible (*negl*) duration.

3.2 Transform Phase

Exaggeration's transform phase converts a comparative analysis problem into a simulation problem by creating a model of the system which has an exaggerated initial value for some parameter. The trick is to produce a description which has a qualitatively different behavior than the original. This is easy for the heat exchanger given the comparative analysis problem "What happens to output temperature if the oil moves faster?" The transform phase produces a description with infinite oil velocity. In general, however, three questions must be answered during the transform process:

- Which parameter should be exaggerated?
- In which direction should the parameter be transformed?
- What should be the final value of the parameter?

The following sections discuss these questions.

3.2.1 Choice of Parameter

For many comparative analysis questions, the question of choice of parameter is easy to answer. Simply transform the parameter that is perturbed in the comparative analysis problem. This approach appears to work whenever the perturbation is a small, differential change.

However, there are slightly different comparative analysis problems in which it is unclear which parameter should be transformed. For example, consider the two heat exchangers shown in figure 3.2. Hot oil is cooled by passing it through a narrow pipe which is in contact with a larger pipe holding cold (but warming) water. The top design has the cold water flowing in the same direction as the hot oil while the bottom design has the two streams running counterflow. An interesting comparative analysis question is "which design can cool the hot oil to a lower temperature?"

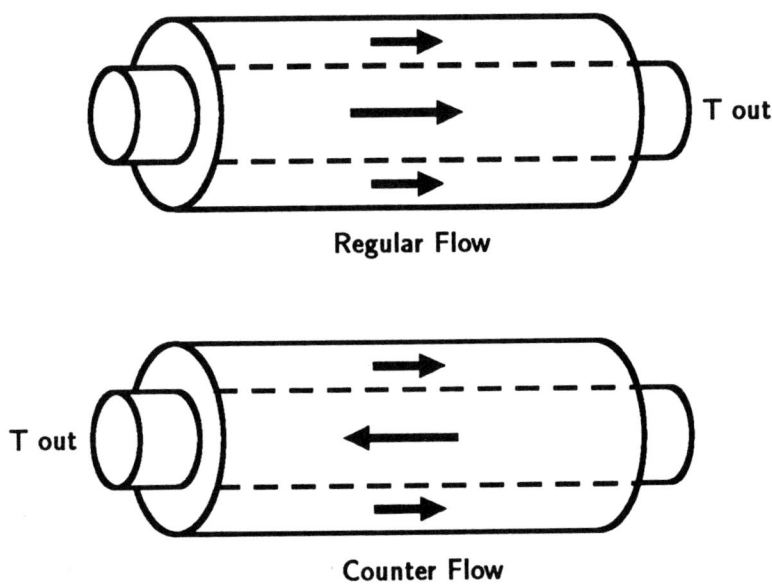

Figure 3.2
Regular and Counter Flow Heat Exchangers

Notice that this question is not of the differential type. The difference between the two designs can not be characterized as an arbitrarily small perturbation. In one case the oil velocity is positive, in the other it is negative; the landmark value, zero, separates the two. As a result, transforming the oil velocity does not result in an answer. If one considers the case in which the oil is moving very slowly, the difference between the two designs vanishes. And if one considers infinite oil velocity, the two designs again act the same—only a negligible amount of heat is lost.

However, if one transforms the pipe length to infinity, then a difference between the designs becomes apparent. In both cases, the oil reaches thermal equilibrium before exiting the pipe. In the case where the oil and coolant flow in the same direction, the equilibrium temperature is intermediate between the oil and water input temperatures. In the counterflow heat exchanger, however, the oil leaves in equilibrium with the fresh cold water entering the exchanger. Thus one can conclude that

3.2. Transform Phase

the counterflow exchanger can cool to a lower temperature.

But how does one know to exaggerate the pipe length? Transforming to an infinite thermal conductivity would have worked just as well, but no other choice results in an answer. Currently, the EXAG program only solves comparative analysis problems with differential perturbations; this counterflow heat exchanger problem would stump it. An interesting direction for future research would be to write a program that transformed every parameter and analyzed the results.[1] While this approach would likely result in many uninteresting transformations, insights like the answer to the counterflow heat exchanger comparison problem would occasionally result as well.

3.2.2 Choice of Direction

When transforming oil velocity to answer the question "What happens to oil output temperature when the flow rate is increased?" EXAG chooses to send the velocity to its limit, infinity, in the direction of the perturbation. This is not the only possibility, however; the following, equally correct, explanation would result if one transformed in the other direction.

> If the oil moved at a negligible rate, then it would take an infinite time to exit the pipe. Thus the oil would have reached thermal equilibrium at the coolant's temperature when it left. Since this is colder than in the finite velocity case, decreasing velocity decreases output temperature and increasing velocity increases output temperature.

There are two criteria for selecting the best direction in which to transform a parameter: ability to get an answer and the intuitive plausibility of the resulting explanation.

Asymmetric Answers While it is usually the case that exaggeration's ability to reach an answer is insensitive to transform direction, this is not always the case. The nondifferential comparative analysis problem of the counterflow heat exchanger (figure 3.2) provides an immediate example. Transforming pipe length to infinity demonstrates the

---
[1] Olivier Raimon has indicated (personal communication) that he is investigating this possibility. He terms the various results 'caricatures' of the original system.

superiority of the counterflow design, but if the pipe length is negligible then there is no difference between the two designs.

Section 3.3.4 explains an asymmetry in the simulation algorithm which partially accounts for this phenomena. In any case, a simple solution is to try transforming in the opposite direction if the first yields no answer.

Psychological Appeal The choice of transformation direction also impacts the intuitive appeal of exaggerated explanations. For example, consider a horizontal, frictionless block oscillating due to the action of a perfect spring. A natural comparative analysis question is "What happens to the period of oscillation if the mass of the block is changed?" Most people find it more convincing to imagine a very heavy block with an infinite period than an incredibly light block with infinitesimal period. Since this effect is psychological, it is very difficult to quantize.[2] As a result, EXAG does not attempt to consider this factor during the transform phase.

3.2.3 Choice of Distance

Once one has chosen a parameter and the direction it should be exaggerated, all that remains to choose is the final value. For most problems, the correct choice is either an infinite or an infinitesimal value, depending on the transform direction. If the trend is towards smaller values, EXAG transforms to infinitesimal values, not to zero. This is the best way to avoid troublesome discontinuities. Section 4.5 talks more about this.

When the trend is toward larger absolute values, EXAG transforms to *inf* or *minf*. For the heat exchanger question "What happens to oil output temperature when flow rate is increased?", positive infinity is a good tation (figure 3.3).

Unfortunately, it is not always appropriate to transform a positive perturbation to infinity. The goal, when choosing a final value, should be to create a new model with asymptotic values that has qualitatively different behavior when simulated. Infinitesimal and infinite values are

---

[2] As Ernie Davis (personal communication) has pointed out, this psychological effect has an interesting physical basis. If the block has negligible mass, then it is dominated by the mass of the spring. The modeling decision that the spring has zero mass become questionable when reasoning about small blocks. After all, a spring with no block attached does not oscillate infinitely fast.

3.2. Transform Phase

$$[X(0)] = (x_0, (inc\ inf))$$
$$[V(0)] = (inf, std)$$
$$[Q(0)] = (q_0, (dec\ fin))$$
$$[F(0)] = (f_0, (inc\ fin))$$
$$[K(0)] = (k_0, std)$$

Figure 3.3
Transform Phase Output

common asymptotes, but not the only ones. Consider the boiler shown in figure 3.4; cold water flows in from the left and steam exits the top.

Given the comparative analysis question, "What happens to the steam output temperature if the water input temperature is increased?" Admittedly, exaggeration is a poor technique for this question;[3] however, as such it is instructive to see how exaggeration must tackle the problem. Indeed, the current implementation, EXAG, does the wrong thing — it transforms the input water temperature upwards to infinity. The upward trend is correct, but infinity is a bad choice of final value. The resulting behavior depends on the details of the boiler model (how are temperature, pressure, and boiling point related?). The possibility exists for one to conclude that the output temperature of the steam would be infinite. Thus one might think that an increase in water temperature leads to an increase in steam temperature when, in fact, the steam temperature does not change.

The reason that this is a poor choice is simple. While an infinite water input temperature does cause asymptotic behavior, it is not the first asymptote reached by increasing water temperature. When the temperature approaches water's boiling point, the boiling rate hits infinity.[4]

In conclusion, the parameter should be transformed the shortest distance that causes some parameter to reach an infinite or infinitesimal value. Frequently, this requires explicitly setting the transformed parameter to a hyperreal value, but not always. For the boiler example, input

---

[3] See section 4 for a discussion of the relative merits of exaggeration and differential qualitative analysis.

[4] This all depends on one's model of boiling. For now, I am assuming the simple model in which boiling rate is proportional to the flame's heat flow and inversely proportional to the difference between water temperature and boiling point. A model which incorporated the latent heat of vaporization would be more complicated.

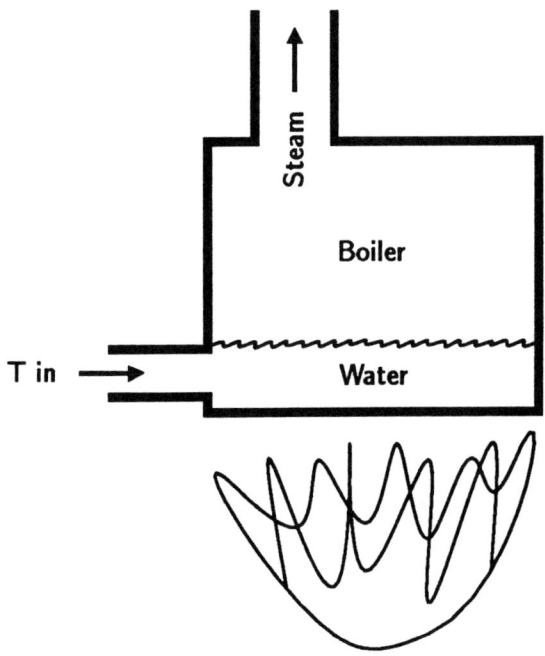

Figure 3.4
A Boiler

temperature should be transformed to the liquid's boiling temperature.

3.3 Simulate Phase

Since the beauty of exaggeration is that it reduces a comparative analysis problem to a problem of qualitative simulation, it should be no surprise that the simulate phase is the most difficult of the three. The trick is to demonstrate a qualitative simulation technique that can handle parameters with infinite and infinitesimal values. Because Kuipers' QSIM [38, 37] is simple, precisely defined and widely available, I chose it as basis for the simulate phase. Sections 5.2 and 4.5 discuss problems with this choice and alternate choices.

Unfortunately, the addition of infinite and infinitesimal values requires

3.3. Simulate Phase

a surprising number of modifications. The fundamental problem is due to the strong reliance that all qualitative simulation algorithms place on the order topology of the standard real numbers [70]; QSIM, for example, assumes that the value spaces of time and the various parameters alternate between open intervals and closed points. Unfortunately, the presence of infinitesimals in the hyperreals results in a more complex topology where this is no longer the case.

The next section briefly reviews QSIM. Then I present the extensions which together form the HR-QSIM algorithm: new transition tables, enhanced constraint filters, the predecessor-persistence filter, the successor-arrival filter, and the irrelevant-transition filter.

3.3.1 How QSIM Works

The following description is simplified from [38]. QSIM takes as input a set of parameters (e.g., heat Q, heat flow F, thermal conductivity K, velocity of the liquid through the pipe V, and position of a unit volume of oil X), a set of equations describing the system (e.g., $V = \frac{d}{dt}X, F = \frac{d}{dt}Q$, and $F = \text{MULT}(Q, K)$), and a set of initial qualitative values for the parameters. As output, QSIM produces a tree of states; each path through the tree represents a possible behavior of the system. The first step of QSIM is to push onto a queue an initial state constructed from the initial conditions. Then the following steps are executed repeatedly until the queue is empty or (or until some arbitrary number of states have been generated).

1. Select a state from the queue.

2. For each parameter in the system, use the parameter's qualitative state (value / derivative pair) as an index into a TRANSITION TABLE. By exploiting the assumption that all parameters are continuously differentiable, transition tables contain only a few next value / derivative pairs for each index. For example, if the representation of a parameter at a time point is 'at the point l_i and *inc*', then in the time interval after the point, the only possible qualitative value is the interval (l_i, l_{i+1}) and the derivative must still be *inc*.

3. For each constraint relating the parameters, generate the set of value / derivative tuples (pairs or triples) by computing the cross

product of the possibilities from step 2. Filter out the tuples whose values or derivatives don't satisfy the constraint.

4. For each pair of constraints that share a parameter, P, check for consistency. If one constraint has a tuple which assigns P a qualitative value / derivative that is consistent with none of the other constraint's tuples, then prune that tuple.

5. Generate all possible global interpretations from the remaining tuples. If interpretations exist, then create new states and make them successors of the existing state.

6. Apply global filtering rules. For example, prune new states that are qualitatively indistinguishable from the previous state. Add the remaining states to the queue.

The next sections explain the substantial modifications necessary to embrace the qualitative representation of the hyperreals. Section 3.3.2 explains how step 2 requires four instead of two transition tables; in addition the choice of table is more complex. Section 3.3.3 discusses the new constraint filters that are necessary for step 3, and shows how one existing filter needs to be modified. The most important change is the addition of temporal filtering, unnecessary in the original QSIM representation. Two kinds of temporal filters are required: predecessor-persistence filtering (section 3.3.4) and successor-arrival filtering (section 3.3.5). Section 3.3.6 introduces several improvements to these techniques.

3.3.2 Transition Tables

The extended qualitative representation requires extensive changes in the use of transition tables. QSIM uses two tables while HR-QSIM needs four. With QSIM it is always obvious which table to use, but this is no longer the case with HR-QSIM. The difference results from the fact that the hyperreals have a different topology than the standard real numbers. However, before considering this difference in detail, it is necessary to understand why QSIM has two tables in the first place.

QSIM Uses Two Different Tables QSIM uses two transition tables to avoid generating inconsistent combinations of transitions that

3.3. Simulate Phase

would need to be filtered later. Because parameters are continuous, certain transitions (i.e. changes in qualitative representation) can't happen at the same time. QSIM uses two tables to group all the compatible state changes together so that these inconsistent transitions are never considered.

For example, consider a system with two parameters, A and B. Let $\mathcal{S}_0$ denote the qualitative state in which $A = (a_0, std)$ and $B = ((b_0, b_1), inc)$. Let $\mathcal{S}_1$ denote the qualitative state in which $A = ((a_0, a_1)inc)$ and $B = (b_1, std)$. Although the change in A's value from $\mathcal{S}_0$ to $\mathcal{S}_1$ is possible and the same is true for B, it is not possible for $\mathcal{S}_0$ to directly precede $\mathcal{S}_1$. In other words the two transitions cannot happen at the same time.

Seeing why this is true requires a rudimentary understanding of the ORDER TOPOLOGY, the study of open and closed sets as defined by the 'less than' inequality [43].

Definition 18 *A set $\mathcal{O}$ of real numbers is* OPEN *if for all x in $\mathcal{O}$ there exists numbers, a and b such that $a < x < b$ and all other numbers y which satisfy $a < y < b$ are members of $\mathcal{O}$. A set $\mathcal{C}$ is* CLOSED *if its complement is open.*[5]

While it is possible for a set to be neither open nor closed, only two sets of standard reals are both open and closed: the empty set and the set of all standard reals. QSIM is concerned with two simple kinds of sets: sets containing a single point, which are always closed, and noninclusive intervals between two points, (a, b), which are always open. In fact, every QSIM behavior is a sequence of states alternating between the state of the system at a closed time point and the state at an open time interval. All this wouldn't matter except that parameters are continuous functions of time. This becomes clear when one considers the general definition of continuity [43] (more general than the familiar epsilon-delta version because it does not depend on standard real values).

Definition 19 *A function $F : \mathcal{X} \to \mathcal{Y}$ is* CONTINUOUS *if and only if for every open subset, $\mathcal{U}$, of $\mathcal{Y}$, the preimage of $\mathcal{U}$, $F^{-1}(\mathcal{U})$, is open.*

This explains why A and B in the example above can't transition at the same time. The qualitative value, a_0, represents a closed set of real

---
[5] Technically, I should be saying "a subset is open *with regard to the whole space*". However, since I will always be considering openness with regard to a whole space and that space is obvious from context, no confusion results from this abbreviation.

numbers, but (b_0, b_1) denotes an open set. Since the parameter B is a continuous function of time, the set of times, $\mathcal{I}_b$, when B has qualitative value, (b_0, b_1), must be open. Similarly, A has value a_0 for a closed set of times, $\mathcal{I}_a$. If state $\mathcal{S}_0$ directly precedes $\mathcal{S}_1$, then $\mathcal{I}_a$ must equal $\mathcal{I}_b$. But this implies that $\mathcal{I}_a$ is both open and closed. Yet we know that $\mathcal{I}_a$ is neither the empty set (since state $\mathcal{S}_0$ exists) nor all of time (since state $\mathcal{S}_1$ exists). Thus $\mathcal{I}_a$ does not equal $\mathcal{I}_b$, i.e. the parameters must transition at different times. This example can be generalized as follows (also see figure 3.5).

Definition 20 *When a parameter transitions from a qualitative representation representing an open set to one denoting a closed set of standard real numbers, the change is called an* OC-TRANSITION. *When the transition is from a closed set to an open set, the event is called a* CO-TRANSITION.[6]

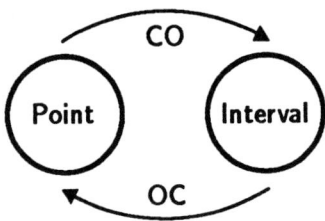

Figure 3.5
Transitions among Standard (QSIM) Qualitative Values

Proposition 13 *Given two adjacent states $\mathcal{S}_i$ and $\mathcal{S}_{i+1}$ in a standard QSIM behavior, if parameters A and B each take on different qualitative representations in the two states, then they both CO-transition or both OC-transition.*

By separating CO-transitions and OC-transitions into two tables, QSIM reduces the number of candidates that get filtered in algorithm stages

---

[6] Kuipers uses the term "I-transition" instead of OC-transitions since they are transitions from an open interval to a closed point. Similarly, he uses the term "P-transition" instead of CO-transitions. Unfortunately, his terminology does not extend well to the hyperreals.

3.3. Simulate Phase

three and four. It is easy to choose the right table to use. If the current state is at a closed time point, then the table of CO-transitions is correct. If the current state is over an open time interval, QSIM selects the table of OC-transitions. As figure 3.6 shows[7] for the single index, (l_i, std), the possible transition given by the two tables are different, but not disjoint. For example, both tables include entries that specify no change. As explained in [69, 38] the mean value theorem and intermediate value theorem of calculus provide the constraint that limits the number of entries in each table.

	CO-transitions	OC-transitions
	(l_i, std)	(l_i, std)
	$((l_i, l_{i+1}), inc)$	
	$((l_{i-1}, l_i), dec)$	

Figure 3.6
QSIM Transition for (l_i, std)

HR-QSIM Needs Four Tables Because the topology of the hyperreals is more complex than that of the standard reals, there are four incompatible types of transitions and thus four transition tables. Two of the tables have the same topology as QSIM's tables. When a parameter changes from a landmark value to the point's halo, it undergoes a CO-transition. The reverse change is an OC-transition. But when a parameter moves between a halo and a standard real interval or between a standard real interval and infinity, the situation gets more complex.

Consider a state change from (HALO 0 +) to $\prec 0$, $inf \succ$. Since there is no largest infinitesimal [49], (HALO 0 +) is an open set. Because there is no smallest positive standard real number, $\prec 0$, $inf \succ$ is also an open set.[8] Thus this transition has a peculiar open-open topology that would be impossible in the standard reals and thus is not considered by QSIM.

The same reasoning that lead to proposition 13 dictates that one of these open-open transitions cannot happen at the same time as a CO-transition or an OC-transition. However, it turns out that there are two

---
[7] This data is based on Table 1 of [38, page 300].
[8] In fact, both these sets are both open and closed—a very different state of affairs from the topology of the standard reals.

incompatible groups of transitions that share the open-open topology.

Definition 21 *When a parameter transitions from one qualitative representation to another* HR-QR *such that its qualitative value changes from a nonstandard open value to a standard open value or its qualitative derivative changes from a negl rate to a fin rate, the event is called an* NS-TRANSITION. *A change in* HR-QR *is called a* SN-TRANSITION *if the opposite change is a NS-transition.*

For example, when a parameter changes from a qualitative value of (HALO l_i +) to $\prec l_i, l_{i+1} \succ$ the change is an NS-transition. If the parameter moved from $\prec 0, inf \succ$ to *inf* then the change would be termed a SN-transition.

Proposition 14 *A NS-transition cannot happen at the same time as a SN-transition.*

Proof: There are several cases to consider. The proof of the first case is taken from Ernie Davis' justification for his temporal topology rule [4].

1. An NS-transition from (HALO 0 +) to $\prec 0, inf \succ$ cannot happen at the same time as an SN-transition from $\prec 0, inf \succ$ to *inf*. Consider a system with three parameters, A, B and C obeying the constraint $C = \text{MULT}(A, B)$. Let S_0 denote a qualitative state in which A has qualitative value (HALO 0 +), and B has value $\prec 0, inf \succ$. Let S_1 denote a qualitative state in which A has qualitative value $\prec 0, inf \succ$ and B has value *inf*. Although the change in A's value from S_0 to S_1 is possible and the same is true for B, it is not possible for S_0 directly precede S_1. Since $C = \text{MULT}(A, B)$, C has qualitative value (HALO 0 +) in state S_0 and *inf* in S_1. Because the continuous parameter C cannot jump between these two values without hitting the intervening values, the two states cannot be adjacent.

2. A NS-transition from (HALO 0 +) to $\prec 0, inf \succ$ cannot happen at the same time as a SN-transition from $\prec 0, inf \succ$ to (HALO 0 +). The previous proof carries if one uses the constraint $A = \text{MULT}(B, C)$.

3. A NS-transition from (HALO l_i +) to $\prec l_i, inf \succ$ cannot happen at the same time as a SN-transition from $\prec 0, inf \succ$ to *inf*. This

3.3. Simulate Phase

is shown by constructing a system which violates case 1 through the use of an ADD constraint. As one parameter transitions from (HALO l_i +) to $\prec l_i$, $inf\succ$, the new parameter transitions from (HALO 0 +) to $\prec 0$, $inf\succ$.

From these base cases, all other situations can be derived □

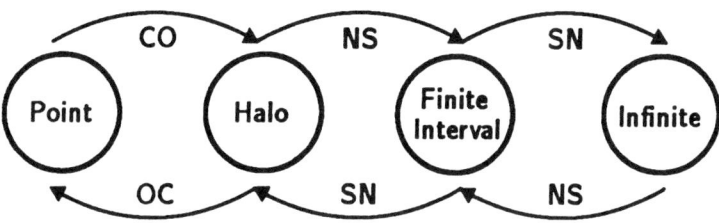

Figure 3.7
Transitions among Qualitative Hyperreal Values

Thus HR-QSIM needs to use four different tables (figure 3.7) to predict possible transitions, one table for each of: CO-transitions, OC-transitions, NS-transitions and SN-transitions. Like the original tables of Williams or Kuipers, the HR-QSIM tables exploit topology, the Mean Value Theorem and the Intermediate Value Theorem. Figure 3.8 shows the table entries which are analogous to the QSIM entries of figure 3.6. The NS and SN entries are not very interesting because the initial value is a closed point which renders impossible any open-open transition topology. Figure ?? shows the possible next HR-QRs for the index ((HALO 0 +), (inc negl)) assuming a quantity space of (minf 0 inf). Entries for other index HR-QRs are similar; space constraints preclude showing them all. In fact, for space reasons, they are implemented procedurally (see appendix D) for the details).

Since QSIM behaviors consist of sequences of states alternating between closed time points and open intervals, the temporal topology uniquely determines which transition table should be used. If the current state is at a closed point, only CO-transitions need be considered. The situation is more complex, however, when performing qualitative simulation using the hyperreals. States can persist for a closed time point, or an open interval of negligible, finite or infinite duration. When a state's

CO-transitions	OC-transitions
(l_i, std)	(l_i, std)
$((HALO\ \ l_i\ +), (inc\ neg))$	
$((HALO\ \ l_i\ -), (dec\ neg))$	

NS-transitions	SN-transitions
(l_i, std)	(l_i, std)

Figure 3.8
Hyperreal Transitions from (l_i, std)

CO-transitions	OC-transitions
$((HALO\ \ 0\ +), (inc\ negl))$	$((HALO\ \ 0\ +), (inc\ negl))$

NS-transitions	SN-transitions
$((HALO\ \ 0\ +), (inc\ negl))$	$((HALO\ \ 0\ +), (inc\ negl))$
$((HALO\ \ 0\ +), (inc\ fin))$	
$(\prec 0, inf\succ, (inc\ fin))$	
$(\prec 0; inf\succ, (inc\ negl))$	

Figure 3.9
Hyperreal Transitions from $((HALO\ \ 0\ +), (inc\ negl))$

temporal topology is open, then three tables must be tried: OC, NS and SN-transitions. As a result, a single state can have two (or more) alternate successor states resulting from different types of transitions. If more than one table predicts the same transition (e.g., no change) then the duplicates are pruned.

Possible Transitions for the Heat Exchanger This section applies the transition tables to the problem of the heat exchanger example. As explained in section 3.2.3 (and figure 3.3), the transform phase generates an initial state that corresponds to a heat exchanger with an infinite rate of fluid flow.

3.3. Simulate Phase

$$[X(0)] = (x_0, (inc\ inf))$$
$$[V(0)] = (inf, std)$$
$$[Q(0)] = (q_0, (dec\ fin))$$
$$[F(0)] = (f_0, (inc\ fin))$$
$$[K(0)] = (k_0, std)$$

The principle of continuity as embodied in the HR-QSIM transition tables greatly limits the set of possible transitions for this state. The independent parameters, V and K, can never change by definition (and thus aren't shown), and the other parameters each have only one possible next HR-QR (from the CO-transition table):

$$[X(\mathcal{A}_1)] = ((\text{HALO}\ x_0\ +), (inc\ inf))$$
$$[Q(\mathcal{A}_1)] = ((\text{HALO}\ q_0\ -), (dec\ fin))$$
$$[F(\mathcal{A}_1)] = ((\text{HALO}\ f_0\ +), (inc\ fin))$$

Since these HR-QRs are determined to be consistent (as described in the next two sections) they define the sole successor to the initial state. This successor state lasts for some (as yet undetermined) interval of time $\mathcal{A}_1$. Next, the transition tables are consulted again; this time the NS- and SN-transition tables produce several possibilities. The NS-transition table allows the following possible HR-QRs:

$$\begin{aligned}
[X(\mathcal{A}_2)] &= ((\text{HALO}\ x_0\ +), (inc\ inf)) && \text{or} \\
& \quad (\prec x_0, 0 \succ, (inc\ inf)) && \text{or} \\
& \quad (\prec x_0, 0 \succ, (inc\ fin)) && \text{or} \\
& \quad ((\text{HALO}\ x_0\ +), (inc\ fin)) \\
[Q(\mathcal{A}_2)] &= ((\text{HALO}\ q_0\ -), (dec\ fin)) && \text{or} \\
& \quad (\prec 0, q_0 \succ, (dec\ fin)) \\
[F(\mathcal{A}_2)] &= ((\text{HALO}\ f_0\ +), (inc\ fin)) && \text{or} \\
& \quad (\prec f_0, 0 \succ, (inc\ fin))
\end{aligned}$$

Since X has four possible HR-QRs, Q has two, and F has two, there are $4 * 2 * 2 = 16$ possible (not necessarily consistent) HR-QR tuples that might form successor states over the time interval $\mathcal{A}_2$. In addition, the SN-transition table admits the following possible HR-QRs:

$$\begin{aligned}
[X(\mathcal{A}_2)] &= ((\text{HALO}\ x_0\ +), (inc\ inf)) \\
[Q(\mathcal{A}_2)] &= ((\text{HALO}\ q_0\ -), (dec\ negl)) && \text{or} \\
& \quad ((\text{HALO}\ q_0\ -), (dec\ fin)) && \text{or} \\
& \quad ((\text{HALO}\ q_0\ -), (dec\ inf)) \\
[F(\mathcal{A}_2)] &= ((\text{HALO}\ f_0\ +), (inc\ negl)) && \text{or} \\
& \quad ((\text{HALO}\ f_0\ +), (inc\ fin)) && \text{or} \\
& \quad ((\text{HALO}\ f_0\ +), (inc\ inf))
\end{aligned}$$

This results in $1 * 3 * 3 = 9$ more HR-QR tuples some of which might form consistent successor states. Since both tables predicted the possibility that all parameters might remain unchanged, the total number of potential, different successor states is $15 + 8 = 23$. These states are not represented explicitly, however, until Waltz filtering has been performed using knowledge of the heat exchanger's structural constraints.

3.3.3 Constraint Filters

Most of the QSIM filters work for the qualitative hyperreal representation without significant changes. The derivative constraint, $V = \frac{d}{dt}(X)$, for example is violated by the NS-transition predictions that X might take on the HR-QDIR of $(inc\ fin)$ since $V = (inf, std)$. Checking this constraint reduces the total space of possible states from 23 to 9.

The type of filtering that requires augmentation is that pertaining to corresponding values. Given a constraint, say $F = \text{MULT}(K, Q)$, and a set of values that are known to fit the constraint, say the initial values f_0, k_0, and q_0, then tuples of values can sometimes be filtered when otherwise they would appear to match the constraint. For example, suppose that QSIM generated the following values: f_0 for F, k_0 for K, and $(0, q_0)$ for Q. Without checking corresponding values, this tuple would seem to satisfy the constraint since the signs, - - +, are acceptable. By checking previously noted values, however, QSIM realizes that this tuple is impossible. It does this by computing the sign of the difference between the proposed values and the known values. This case is inconsistent [38], but if F had the interval value, $(f_0, 0)$, then the differences would have been acceptable.

In adapting this algorithm to the hyperreal representation, some changes are necessary. In addition to checking the sign of the difference between proposed and known corresponding values, HR-QSIM also checks the order of magnitude of the distance as well. Thus the F-K-Q-tuple, (HALO f_0 +), k_0, $\prec 0, q_0 \succ$, is eliminated even though the signs of the differences are satisfactory. It is important to realize that *inf* and *minf* are not like normal landmark values; they each represent a whole interval of hyperreal numbers. As a result, corresponding values that include an infinity are never unique, hence less useful for filtering. Filtering HR-QR tuples with inconsistent corresponding values reduces the number of possible states from 9 to 5.

In addition to these checks on the order of magnitude of parame-

3.3. Simulate Phase

ters that are related by a constraint, it is useful to check the order of magnitude of the qualitative derivatives of parameters involved in a constraint. Again consider the constraint $F = \text{MULT}(K, Q)$ and suppose that the qualitative derivative of F is $(inc, negl)$ and that of K is std, then the qualitative derivative of Q must be $(dec, negl)$. However, if the heat exchanger had infinite thermal conductivity, i.e. K were $minf$ then the situation would be more complicated. HR-QSIM uses a qualitative version of the rule:

$$\tfrac{d}{dt}(FG) = F\tfrac{d}{dt}G + G\tfrac{d}{dt}F$$

This rule reduces the number of possible new successor states from 5 to 3.[9]

Either X transitions to $\prec x_0, 0 \succ$ while Q and F remain in their halos:

$$\begin{aligned}
{[X(\mathcal{A}_2)]} &= (\prec x_0, 0\succ, (inc\ inf)) \\
{[Q(\mathcal{A}_2)]} &= ((\text{HALO}\ q_0\ -), (dec\ fin)) \\
{[F(\mathcal{A}_2)]} &= ((\text{HALO}\ f_0\ +), (inc\ fin))
\end{aligned}$$

Or Q and F transition out of their halos while X remains in its:

$$\begin{aligned}
{[X(\mathcal{A}_2)]} &= ((\text{HALO}\ x_0\ +), (inc\ inf)) \\
{[Q(\mathcal{A}_2)]} &= (\prec 0, q_0\succ, (dec\ fin)) \\
{[F(\mathcal{A}_2)]} &= (\prec f_0, 0\succ, (inc\ fin))
\end{aligned}$$

Or all three parameters transition out of their halos:

$$\begin{aligned}
{[X(\mathcal{A}_2)]} &= ((\text{HALO}\ x_0\ +), (inc\ inf)) \\
{[Q(\mathcal{A}_2)]} &= ((\text{HALO}\ q_0\ -), (dec\ fin)) \\
{[F(\mathcal{A}_2)]} &= ((\text{HALO}\ f_0\ +), (inc\ fin))
\end{aligned}$$

The next sections explains how HR-QSIM uses the predecessor-persistence and successor-arrival filters to determine that only the first of these possibilities is reasonable.

---

[9] The relative power of these filtering rules is skewed by the order of application. Whichever filter is applied first usually culls out the greatest number of inconsistent possibilities. A more accurate metric is the increased number of possible successors when a given filter is turned off.

3.3.4 Predecessor-Persistence Filter

The final extensions have to do with time. QSIM's temporal representation is simple: states persist for either an instant (a closed point of time) or a finite open interval. Furthermore, QSIM can quickly tell how long any state will last; if the predecessor state lasted for an instant, the successor will persist for an interval and vice versa. The situation is not so simple for HR-QSIM. Since the qualitative hyperreal representation allows derivatives to have a negligible order of magnitude, a state might last for an infinite time before a parameter transitioned to a new landmark value. And if some parameter had an *inf* derivative, then the state might persist for only a negligible time. Since the original QSIM cases are also still possible, I distinguish between the following four qualitative lengths of time: 0, *negl*, *fin*, and *inf*. HR-QSIM uses two techniques, predecessor-persistence filtering and successor-arrival filtering (section 3.3.5), to deduce the temporal extent of qualitative states and to prune inconsistent successors during simulation.

The difference between the two techniques results from the following interesting observaton about transitions in the qualitative hyperreal representation:

> It may take longer for a parameter to transition to a new qualitative value than it spends in its old value.

This curious state of affairs stems from the fact that the hyperreals do not have the least-upper bound property — there is neither a smallest positive standard real nor a largest positive infinitesimal.[10] The following concrete example (recapitulated from section 1.5.3) makes this clear.

Let P be a parameter, in other words a function from the hyperreals to the hyperreals, defined as the identity function $P(t) = t$ (figure 3.10). Consider the set of times that the qualitative value, (*halo* 0 +) accurately describes P (below I formalize this notion as the "persistence of a parameter's value"). I claim that P persists in (*halo* 0 +) for a negligible length of time. One can derive a contradiction otherwise. For example, if P persists in the halo for a standard finite time, t_0, then that would imply that $t_0 \in$ (HALO 0+) in other words that t_0 is an infinitesimal.

---
[10] Mathematically oriented readers may consider the analogous topology of R^2 under a lexicographic ordering.

3.3. Simulate Phase   85

This contradicts the assumption that t_0 was a standard finite number. Persistence values of *inf* and 0 also result in contradictions. Thus P maintains the value of (HALO 0 +) for *negl* time.

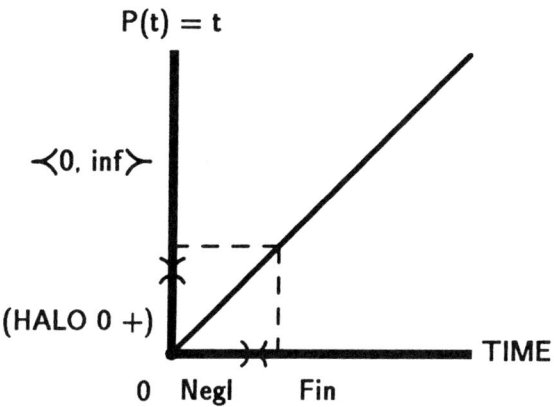

Figure 3.10
The Difference Between Peristence and Arrival Times

Now consider the time it takes for P to reach the qualitative value, $\prec 0, inf \succ$. The next section formalizes this notion as 'successor-arrival time'; here I argue informally that P's successor-arrival time is *fin*. By definition of $\prec 0, inf \succ$, when P reaches this qualitative value it must have taken a standard real value, r_0. Thus r_0 time must have elapsed since P left 0. Of course, P must reach $\frac{r_0}{2}$ before r_0, so it might appear natural approach to define successor arrival time in terms of the greatest-lower bound of these elapsed times. Unfortunately, this approach does not work — the hyperreals have is no greatest-lower bound for the set of positive noninfinitesimal numbers. Intuitively, there are two choices for a qualitative value of successor arrival time: *fin* and *negl*. But *negl* does not capture the meaning of arrival since $P(t_1) \notin \prec 0, inf \succ$ for any infinitesimal t_1. Thus it must take *fin* time for P to arrive at a $\prec 0, inf \succ$ from 0. And since only *negl* time passed reaching (HALO 0 +) from 0, P must take *fin-negl=fin* time to arrive at this new qualitative value from (HALO 0 +). [11] But this means that P takes longer to reach

---
[11] This is all justified formally in the remainder of this section and in section 3.3.5.

its new value than it spends in its original value. Remember that this is true even though there is no intervening hyperreal value sandwiched between (HALO 0 +) and $\prec 0, inf\succ$.

Several benefits result from considering persistence and arrival temporal measures separately. The relationship between the time when one state ends and another starts is made clear. The resulting theory of hyperreal simulation is clean, even if unintuitive. Finally, an effective algorithm results. The remainder of this section concerns predecessor-persistence filtering, a technique for eliminating impossible successor states by checking persistence times. Section 3.3.5 deals with the related technique, the successor-arrival filter. Both techniques use a common mechanism, the DISTANCE-RATE-TIME TABLE to compute temporal values. This table is indexed by rate and distance values and returns a time value. In both cases, the rate expressions come directly from the order of magnitude of the parameter's qualitative derivative. The difference between the time a parameter will persist in its current value and the time required to reach its successor value comes from the distance used to index into the table. To calculate the time a parameter can persist in a qualitative value, the 'width' of the qualitative value is used as a table index.

Width of a Qualitative Value Intuitively, the width of a qualitative value is the order of magnitude of the maximum distance between any two members of the set of hyperreal points that underlie the qualitative value.

Definition 22 *Let P be a parameter and Γ be a qualitative hyperreal value of P. Define the set of hyperreal points of Γ as*

POINTS$(\Gamma) \equiv \{p | P(t) = p \Rightarrow$ HR-QVAL$(P(t)) = \Gamma\}$

Define the WIDTH *of a qualitative value, Γ, as the maximum element of the set:*

$\{$OM$(|v - u|) \mid \forall v, u \in$ POINTS$(\Gamma)\}$

A maximum value exists for this set, since it has at most four members: 0, *negl*, *fin*, and *inf*.[12] This definition yields the following intuitive

---
[12]It is important to compute the maximum after computing the order of magnitudes, rather than the order of magnitude of the largest value, since no maximum or least-upper bound for $|v - u|$ need exist.

3.3. Simulate Phase

result:

Proposition 15 *Let Γ be the qualitative hyperreal value of a parameter. If Γ is a landmark point, then* WIDTH$(\Gamma) = 0$. *If Γ is the halo of a landmark, then* WIDTH$(\Gamma) =$ negl. *If Γ is either inf or minf, then* WIDTH$(\Gamma) =$ inf. *Otherwise* WIDTH$(\Gamma) =$ fin.

By using these width values as an index to the distance-rate-time table (figure 3.11), HR-QSIM calculates how long each parameter can persist in its current qualitative value.

Distance-Rate-Time Table The distance-rate-time table (figure 3.11) determines the length of time it takes to go some distance at a given rate. An entry of '?' in the table indicates that *inf, fin, negl*, or 0 time may elapse (but see the improvements in section 3.3.6). When calculating the time that a parameter will persist in a qualitative value, the order of magnitude of the parameter's derivative and the width of the qualitative value are used as indices.

		Distance			
		inf	fin	negl	0
	inf	?	negl	negl	0
Rate	fin	inf	fin	negl	0
	negl	inf	inf	?	0

Figure 3.11
The Distance-Rate-Time Table

Predecessor-Persistence Filtering HR-QSIM calculates persistence values for two reasons. From the persistences of each parameter, one can determine how long a qualitative state is a valid description of a system. Secondly, by comparing the persistences of all the parameters in a system, one can often filter out inconsistent transitions that were not eliminated by the transition tables or constraint filters. Since the heat exchanger does not provide a good illustration, consider the following simple example.

Suppose the two parameters, X and Y, are both increasing at the same *fin* rate, and this rate is held constant. In the predecessor state,

X has the landmark value, 0, and Y has the (HALO 0 $-$) as its value. Constraint filtering leaves three sets of possible transitions:

Either X transitions off 0 before Y changes to 0:

$$[X(\mathcal{A}_{i+1})] = ((\text{HALO } 0\ +), (\text{inc fin}))$$
$$[Y(\mathcal{A}_{i+1})] = ((\text{HALO } 0\ -), (\text{inc fin}))$$

Or Y reaches 0 before X leaves 0:

$$[X(\mathcal{A}_{i+1})] = (0, (\text{inc fin}))$$
$$[Y(\mathcal{A}_{i+1})] = (0, (\text{inc fin}))$$

Or they both transition at the same time:

$$[X(\mathcal{A}_{i+1})] = ((\text{HALO } 0\ +), (\text{inc fin}))$$
$$[Y(\mathcal{A}_{i+1})] = (0, (\text{inc fin}))$$

The question is, which of these successor states is possible? The answer comes from analyzing the persistence of the predecessor state. The width of X's qualitative value is 0 and X is moving with *fin* speed, so the distance-rate-time table lists X's persistence as 0. Y has the same rate and has *negl* width, so Y's persistence is *negl*. This means that Y must persist in its qualitative value for longer than X. In other words, X must transition before Y and only the first of the three transition sets shown above is consistent.

The general predecessor-persistence filtering algorithm is shown below. Inputs are two sets: parameter HR-QRs in the predecessor state and HR-QRs for the proposed successor state. Output is a set of possible persistences for the predecessor state or the empty set if the proposed successor is inconsistent.

1. Set SP = the set $\{0, negl, fin, inf\}$.

2. For each parameter, X

    (a) Using X's speed and the width of its value in the predecessor state, let P = the set of X's possible persistences from the distance-rate-time table.

    (b) If X transitions from one qualitative state to another from the predecessor to the successor states, set SP = SP intersect P.

3.3. Simulate Phase

(c) Otherwise, if X has the same qualitative value, HR-QVAL, in the predecessor and successor states, remove any time values from SP that are greater than the largest value in P.

3. If SP is empty, the successor state is inconsistent, otherwise SP is the set of possible persistences for the predecessor state.

3.3.5 Successor-Arrival Filter

Like persistence values, arrival times are both intrinsically interesting and useful as a means for eliminating inconsistent transitions that have escaped the scythe of other filters. This section discusses how arrival times are used in filtering; see section 3.4.1 for an explanation of how the scale phase uses arrival values to answer comparative analysis questions.

Successor-arrival filtering is very similar to predecessor-persistence filtering. Both compute a qualitative length, width and distance respectively, and use it as an index to the distance-rate-time table (figure 3.11). Likewise, both techniques use individual parameter times to narrow the range of allowable times for the state transition as a whole. The difference between the two techniques results from a different focus: on the predecessor state for persistence filtering and on the successor state for arrival filtering.

Distance Between Qualitative Values Calculating the time that a parameter takes to arrive at a new qualitative value from an old one requires a notion of the distance between the two different values. Intuitively, the distance between two qualitative values is the order of magnitude of the minimum distance between any two points in the hyperreal sets underlying the two qualitative values.

Definition 23 *Let P be a parameter and let Γ and Σ be qualitative hyperreal values of P. Define the* DISTANCE *between Γ and Σ as the minimum element of the set:*

$$\{\text{OM}(|v - u|) \mid \forall v \in \text{POINTS}(\Gamma) \; \forall u \in \text{POINTS}(\Sigma)\}$$

As with the definition of width, it is important that the minimum operator is applied *after* converting hyperreal differences into order of magnitudes. As one would hope, this definition of distance behaves as required for a metric [50]; it is symmetric, obeys the triangle inequality[13], and the distance from one qualitative value to itself is guaranteed to be zero.

Proposition 16 *Let Γ and Σ be qualitative hyperreal values of a parameter. If Γ is a landmark point and Σ is one of the halos of the landmark, then* DISTANCE$(\Gamma, \Sigma) = negl$. *If Γ is a halo and Σ is an adjacent finite interval, then* DISTANCE$(\Gamma, \Sigma) = fin$. *Finally,* DISTANCE$(\prec l_i, inf\succ, inf) = inf$.

Thus the width of a halo is *negl* while the distance from the halo to a neighboring finite interval is *fin*. This leads to the conclusion that a parameter starting from 0 with *fin* speed may spend *negl* time in (HALO 0 +), yet take *fin* time to reach $\prec 0, inf \succ$.

Successor-Arrival Filtering The successor-arrival filtering algorithm is an enhancement on the predecessor-persistence filter. The inputs are parameter HR-QRs for the predecessor and proposed successor states. If the successor state is consistent, then sets of possible persistence and arrival times are output. The trick is to restrict the state arrival time, SA, with the persistence value of an unchanging parameter and with the arrival value of a parameter that changes.

1. Set SP = the set $\{0, negl, fin, inf\}$.

2. Set SA = the set $\{negl, fin, inf\}$.

3. For each parameter, X

    (a) Using X's speed and the width of its qualitative value in the predecessor state, let P = the set of X's possible persistences from the distance-rate-time table.

    (b) Using X's speed and the distance from its qualitative value in the predecessor state to its value in the successor state, let A = the set of X's possible arrivals from the distance-rate-time table.

    (c) If X transitions from one qualitative value to another from the predecessor to the successor states,

---

[13] The distance between a and b plus the distance between b and c is greater or equal to the distance between a and c.

3.3. Simulate Phase

- Set SP = SP intersect P.
- Set SA = SA intersect A.

(d) Otherwise, if X has the same qualitative value in the two states,

- Remove any time values from SP that are greater than the largest value in P.
- Remove any time values from SA that are greater than the largest value in P (not A! Since this parameter is not changing, the next state must arrive while this parameter is still persisting).

4. See section 3.3.6 page 96 for an extra step.

5. If SP or SA is empty, the successor state is inconsistent, otherwise SP and SA are the sets of possible persistences and arrivals respectively.

Heat Exchanger Example The heat exchanger example provides a nice illustration of successor-arrival filtering. Recall that the transform phase gave the initial state the following HR-QRs:

$$[X(0)] = (x_0, (inc\ inf))$$
$$[V(0)] = (inf, std)$$
$$[Q(0)] = (q_0, (dec\ fin))$$
$$[F(0)] = (f_0, (inc\ fin))$$
$$[K(0)] = (k_0, std)$$

This state can persist for only a point of time (denoted 0) because several parameters are moving from landmarks. The second state arrives in *negl* time and has new HR-QRs for X, Q, and F:

$$[X(\mathcal{A}_1)] = ((\text{HALO}\ x_0\ +), (inc\ inf))$$
$$[Q(\mathcal{A}_1)] = ((\text{HALO}\ q_0\ -), (dec\ fin))$$
$$[F(\mathcal{A}_1)] = ((\text{HALO}\ f_0\ +), (inc\ fin))$$

Recall that the constraint filters were unable to choose between three possible successors of this state. The question was whether X would transition from its halo before, after or at the same time as Q and F transitioned from their halo. Since each parameter is in a halo, each has a qualitative width of *negl*, and since each is moving towards a finite interval, each parameter must travel a *fin* distance before transitioning. Plugging these values into the distance-rate-time table leads to the conclusion that every parameter has a persistence value of *negl*. Since all parameters have the same persistence value, the state as a whole has that persistence: $|\mathcal{A}_1| = negl$.

Using distance as an index to the distance-rate-time table shows that X has a *negl* arrival value, but Q and F have *fin* arrival values. Successor-arrival filtering uses these values to keep only those successor states in which X transitions before Q and F. For example, consider the successor in which all three transition at the same time. This candidate would have the following HR-QRs:

$$[X(\mathcal{A}_2)] = (\prec x_0, 0 \succ, (inc\ inf))$$
$$[Q(\mathcal{A}_2)] = (\prec 0, q_0 \succ, (dec\ fin))$$
$$[F(\mathcal{A}_2)] = (\prec f_0, 0 \succ, (inc\ fin))$$

Since both X and Q have transitioned, SA = the intersection of the sets of their arrival times: $\{negl\} \cap \{fin\} = \emptyset$. Thus this successor is inconsistent. Now suppose that Q and F transition before X; the successor state would have the following HR-QRs:

$$[X(\mathcal{A}_2)] = ((\text{HALO}\ x_0+), (inc\ inf))$$
$$[Q(\mathcal{A}_2)] = (\prec 0, q_0 \succ, (dec\ fin))$$
$$[F(\mathcal{A}_2)] = (\prec f_0, 0 \succ, (inc\ fin))$$

Since Q is transitioning, SA is set to its initial value intersected by the set of Q's arrival times; thus SA = $\{fin\}$. But since X isn't changing, the successor state's arrival time must be less than X's largest persistence value, *negl*, so *fin* is not acceptable. Once again, no arrival time makes sense for this successor state so the successor is inconsistent. The only set of transitions that pass the test are the following; they arrive in *negl* time.

$$[X(\mathcal{A}_2)] = (\prec x_0, 0 \succ, (inc\ inf))$$
$$[Q(\mathcal{A}_2)] = ((\text{HALO}\ q_0-), (dec\ fin))$$
$$[F(\mathcal{A}_2)] = ((\text{HALO}\ f_0+), (inc\ fin))$$

Since X's distance is still *fin*, similar reasoning holds again. This state persists for *negl* time until X transitions to (HALO 0 −) and then to 0 (always arriving in *negl* time) while Q and F remain in the halo of their original landmark values. Note the central role of persistence

3.3. Simulate Phase

calculations and successor-arrival filtering in ensuring the correct result for exaggeration. While the enhanced transition tables and constraint filtering are also important, persistence and arrival filtering are responsible for deducing that negligible heat is lost when oil moves infinitely fast through a heat exchanger.

3.3.6 Improving the Temporal Filters

Although the distance-rate-time table as shown in figure 3.11 is sufficient to disambiguate the behavior of the infinite velocity heat exchanger, the ambiguity resulting from *inf* rate and *inf* distance is a major liability in many other examples. For example, consider a block attached to a stretched spring on a frictionless, horizontal surface and the comparative analysis question "What happens to the period of oscillation when the spring is made more stiff?"

Since the period decreases, we would like exaggeration to be able to conclude that a system with *inf* spring constant will have a period of *negl* duration. However, this is impossible using the distance-rate-time table above. The first step is easy—since $K = minf$ an infinite force is applied, and the equation $F = MA$ requires that acceleration be infinite. The question is how long will it take before V arrives at *inf*? Since V is initially zero, it has an infinite distance to travel, yet its derivative, A, is also *inf*. The ambiguity of the persistence table shown above precludes an answer. One would like to conclude that it will only take *negl* time for V to reach infinity, because then even the distance-rate-time table above could conclude that X will travel the finite distance to its rest position in *negl* time. If it took longer than *negl* time for V to transition to *inf*, say *fin* time, then it would take at least *fin* time for X to reach rest position, and the scale phase would be unable to definitively answer the comparative analysis question.

Moving Infinitely Far, Infinitely Fast In fact, it is possible to eliminate the ambiguity from the distance-rate-time table *inf* divided by *inf* entry, in exactly half the cases. The determinant is the direction of travel. There are only two ways that a parameter can transition after travelling an infinite distance—it must be moving from *inf* or *minf* to a finite value or vice versa. If the parameter is moving infinitely fast towards an infinite value, then the transition will occur in *negl* time, otherwise it could take *negl*, *fin*, or even *inf* time.

Proposition 17 Infinite-Distance Arrival Rule

Let S_i and S_{i+1} be adjacent hyperreal qualitative states in a behavior. Let P be a parameter. If P has a finite value in S_i and an infinite value in S_{i+1} and if P's qualitative derivative has order of magnitude $\text{OM} = \inf$ in S_i, then P has *negl* arrival time; after *negl* time, P will have reached an infinite value.

Proof: Since the width of P's qualitative value is *fin*, P has *negl* persistence. Let t_0 be one of the time points in this open interval of *negl* persistence. Let R be a parameter defined as:

$$R(t) = t - t_0$$

Since t_0 was chosen from an open interval, there are times when P has a finite value and R has a negligible value. Now consider which parameter transitions first: R moving to a finite value or P moving to an infinite one?

Since R's change is an NS-transition and P's is a SN-transition, proposition 14 states that they cannot happen together. Furthermore, R cannot transition before P since R has an arrival time of *fin* while P's persistence time is *negl*. Thus P must transition before R. In other words,

$\exists t_1$ such that $\text{HR-QVAL}(P(t_1)) = \inf \ \wedge \ \text{HR-QVAL}(R(t_1)) = (\text{HALO} \ \ 0 \ +)$

Thus by definition of R and $(\text{HALO} \ \ 0 \ +)$,

$$\text{OM}(t_1 - t_0) = negl$$

So P must arrive in *negl* time □

This rule is both surprising and important to exaggeration's success. As the spring example hinted, a number of exaggerated systems have transitions that access the *inf* divided by *inf* entry in the persistence table. Without the disambiguation provided by the infinite arrival rule, exaggeration would solve fewer comparative analysis problems.

In case the preceding proof seems obscure, the remainder of this section contains an intuitive justification of the rule that should clarify the underlying phenomena. In addition, I explain why the rule doesn't apply to parameters transitioning in the reverse direction.

3.3. Simulate Phase

Let $\frac{d}{dt}P = inf$ and let P transition from a finite value to inf. There are three cases: the arrival time could be $negl$, fin, or inf. Suppose that it doesn't take $negl$ time. Perhaps instead it takes fin time to transition to infinity. Then P doesn't take on an infinite value until some standard finite time, t_0, has passed. Then after time $\frac{t_0}{2}$, P must still have a finite value. But this means that even though P has been traveling at infinite speed for finite time $\frac{t_0}{2}$, it has only gone finite distance. This contradicts the P persistence value from the original table. The other possibility also produces a contradiction. If it takes infinite time for P to reach an infinite value, then P will again have traveled at most finite distance after finite time. The only consistent possibility is that the transition happens in $negl$ time. Of course, this is only a sketchy argument, but it illuminates the formal proof.

Note that the argument does not work when P is transitioning from inf to a finite value. Transitions in this direction can take $negl$, fin, or even inf time to arrive. For example, suppose P takes the finite time, t_0, to reach a finite value from inf. What is P's value after time $\frac{t_0}{2}$? It is perfectly consistent that P still be inf. By time $\frac{t_0}{2}$, P's underlying hyperreal value could have changed an infinite amount without a change in qualitative value because the inf qualitative value has an infinite width and thus an arbitrary persistence.[14]

Moving Negligibly Far, Negligibly Fast It is also possible to restrict the possible times taken to traverse a $negl$ distance at $negl$ speed. For example, suppose parameter P is at landmark p_0 and increasing with $negl$ rate. The distance-rate-time table shows that its persistence must be 0, but its arrival time for the successor value (HALO p_0 +) is ambiguous since $negl$ distance is traversed at $negl$ speed. In fact, the arrival time cannot be fin or inf— it must be $negl$. Suppose that the arrival time was fin, that means that fin time elapses before P takes on a value in (HALO p_0 +), but this leaves $negl$ time unaccounted for. What value did R take for these times? Since there are no values between p_0 and (HALO p_0 +), an arrival value of fin or inf results in a contradiction.

The reverse case results when P has qualitative value (HALO p_0 +) and is increasing towards $\prec p_0$, $inf \succ$ with $negl$ rate. Since the distance

---

[14] The actual proof cannot be reversed for a similar reason. If P is moving from an infinite to a finite value then the initial state's persistence value is not guaranteed to be $negl$. Thus one cannot conclude that P transitions before R.

between values is *fin*, the arrival time is *inf*. The distance-rate-time table, however, is ambiguous regarding *P*'s persistence value: *negl*, *fin*, and *inf* are all listed as possible. In fact, *negl* is impossible since that would leave *fin* time unaccounted. *P*'s arrival value must be either *inf* or *fin*. The following proposition generalizes these cases.

Proposition 18 Temporal Continuity Rule

The time for a state S_i to arrive at a successor S_{i+1} can never be less than the persistence of S_i. In addition, the arrival time can not be more than one order of magnitude larger than the persistence time.

This rule is implemented as an enhancement to the predecessor-persistence / successor-arrival algorithm (page 91):

4. Remove any values from SA that are more than one order of magnitude greater than the largest value of SP. Remove any values of SP that are more than one order of magnitude smaller than the smallest element of SA.

3.3.7 Irrelevant-Transition Filter

For many examples, the transition tables and filters described above are sufficient to enable qualitative simulation. Some examples, however, cause intractable branching if just these filters are used. In these cases, most every state has several successor states; the result is an exponential number of predicted behaviors. Close inspection of these cases reveals that many of the transitions are irrelevant — they do not affect observable quantities. In fact, almost all intractable branching is caused by predicted changes in the order of magnitude of the HR-QDIR of the highest order derivative in the system.[15]

For example, consider the spring / block system with negligible mass. Position is initially steady at the landmark x_0, velocity has a HR-QR of $(0, (inc\ inf))$ and acceleration has a HR-QR of (inf, std). There is only one successor:

$$[X(\mathcal{A}_1)] = ((\text{HALO}\ \ x_0\ +), (inc\ negl))$$
$$[V(\mathcal{A}_1)] = ((\text{HALO}\ \ 0\ +), (inc\ inf))$$
$$[A(\mathcal{A}_1)] = (inf, (dec\ negl))$$

---

[15] This is similar to the problem of 'chatter' dedcribed by Kuipers and Chiu in [40].

3.3. Simulate Phase

V will only take *negl* time to arrive at its successor value, $\prec 0, inf \succ$, and once it does, a single unbranching behavior will take velocity to *inf* and position to zero. Unfortunately, it is perfectly consistent that before V reaches $\prec 0, inf \succ$, A could change qualitative derivatives (*dec negl*) to (*dec fin*) to (*dec inf*) back to (*dec fin*) and so on, all in *negl* time. Since each of these states lasts for *negl* time, the changes have little physical significance.

Of course, one cannot simply ban successor states that differ only in the order of magnitude of some parameter's derivative — sometimes these transitions are necessary to enable a later change that is physically significant. The trick is to filter only the transitions which are guaranteed to be irrelevant. For example above, it is reasonable to allow A to change from (*dec negl*) to (*dec fin*) to (*dec inf*) since each of these derivative values might enable an interesting successor. But when A tries to switch back to (*dec fin*), it is reasonable to blow the whistle. A successor that repeats this previous state cannot be a useful.

In general, the irrelevant-transition filter compares a candidate successor state with the immediately preceding states. If the candidate is equal to a previous state and all intervening states differ only in the order of magnitude values of parameter derivatives, then the candidate is eliminated. This approach does not disconnect any possible states. If a qualitative state, S_i, is part of a behavior that fails to satisfy the filter, then there is guaranteed to be a behavior that includes S_i and satisfies the filter. Without using the irrelevant-transition filter, exaggeration would solve far fewer problems.

3.3.8 Summary

Exaggeration largely reduces a comparative analysis problem to the problem of simulating a system with parameters using a qualitative hyperreal representation. Since comparative analysis is a challenging task, one should not be surprised that the process of hyperreal qualitative simulation is difficult. This section described one way to build such a simulator. QSIM was taken as the base for exaggeration's simulate phase, because of its availability, efficiency and precise specification. However, the techniques described in this section, are applicable to all qualitative simulation approaches:

- Exploiting hyperreal continuity, by distinguishing OC-, CO-, NS-, and SN-transitions,

- Enforcing order of magnitude consistency in corresponding values and derivatives,

- Predecessor-persistence filtering with the width of predecessor qualitative values as an index to the distance-rate-time-table,

- Successor-arrival filtering with the distance between predecessor and successor qualitative values as an index, and the

- Infinite-distance arrival rule to disambiguate the distance-rate-time table,

The computational complexity of exaggeration in general and the simulate phase in particular is addressed in section 4.4. The possible advantages of other approaches to qualitative simulation are discussed in section 5. The next section concludes the basic presentation of the exaggeration algorithm by describing how the scale phase interprets the simulate phase results to answer comparative analysis questions.

3.4 Scale Phase

The scale phase answers comparative analysis questions by comparing a standard behavior of the original system (figure 3.12)[16] with the hyperreal behavior (figure 3.13) that HR-QSIM produces from the transformed initial conditions. If the behaviors are qualitatively different, i.e. have different qualitative values, then the comparative analysis question can often be answered.

The scale phase's first task is to choose what to compare in the two behaviors; this depends on the specific comparative analysis question. If the question is one of a parameter's relative change value at an event, the scale phase must match events. If the question concerns the duration of a time interval, then the scale phase must match events that start and end the interval. In both cases, an abstract description of corresponding events is required. In the EXAG implementation this description is simply the conjunction of partial specifications for the HR-QRs of one or

---

[16] This figure uses square brackets to denote QSIM's qualitative representation, not the hyperreal qualitative representation.

3.4. Scale Phase

$State\, \mathcal{S}_1:$ $\quad [X(0)] = (x_0, inc)$
$\quad\quad\quad\quad\;\; [Q(0)] = (q_0, dec)$
$\quad\quad\quad\quad\;\; [F(0)] = (f_0, inc) \quad\quad$ Persistence: 0

$State\, \mathcal{S}_2:$ $\quad [X((0,t_1))] = ((x_0, 0), inc)$
$\quad\quad\quad\quad\;\; [Q((0,t_1))] = ((0, q_0), dec)$
$\quad\quad\quad\quad\;\; [F((0,t_1))] = ((f_0, 0), inc) \quad$ Persistence: fin

$State\, \mathcal{S}_3:$ $\quad [X(t_1)] = (0, inc)$
$\quad\quad\quad\quad\;\; [Q(t_1)] = ((0, q_0), dec)$
$\quad\quad\quad\quad\;\; [F(t_1)] = ((f_0, 0), inc) \quad$ Persistence: 0

Figure 3.12
Behavior of a Standard Heat Exchanger

more parameters. For example, one can specify the event when the hot oil exits the heat exchanger by specifying that X equals the landmark zero. By leaving its qualitative derivative unspecified, this description specifies a qualitative state in both the original and exaggerated behaviors, ($\mathcal{S}_3$) and ($\mathcal{S}_e$) respectively.

Since the comparative analysis question asked what happens to the heat of the oil as it exits, the qualitative value of parameter Q is now compared in the two states. In $\mathcal{S}_3$, $Q = (0, q_0)$ while $Q = (\text{HALO}\;\; q_0\; -)$ in the $\mathcal{S}_e$; thus heat is greater in the exaggerated behavior. Since an extreme increase in velocity caused a noticeable increase in output heat, the scale phase concludes that any increase in velocity will cause some increase in output heat. While this conclusion is not guaranteed sound, it is frequently correct. Section 4.3.1 explains the conditions that cause faulty predictions, while the rest of this section considers two remaining details in the scale phase algorithm: questions about durations and cases when the simulate phase predicts more than one possible exaggerated behavior.

3.4.1 Scaling Durations

Answering comparative analysis questions about changes in the time duration between two events requires the ability to measure lengths of behavioral fragments for standard and exaggerated systems. Recall that

$$
\begin{aligned}
State\, \mathcal{S}_a: \quad & [X(0)] && = && (x_0, (inc\ inf)) \\
& [Q(0)] && = && (q_0, (dec\ fin)) \\
& [F(0)] && = && (f_0, (inc\ fin)) && \text{Persistence:} && 0 \\
& && && && \text{Arrival:} && negl \\
State\, \mathcal{S}_b: \quad & [X(\mathcal{A}_b)] && = && ((\text{HALO}\ x_0\ +), (inc\ inf)) \\
& [Q(\mathcal{A}_b)] && = && ((\text{HALO}\ q_0\ -), (dec\ fin)) \\
& [F(\mathcal{A}_b)] && = && ((\text{HALO}\ f_0\ +), (inc\ fin)) && \text{Persistence:} && negl \\
& && && && \text{Arrival:} && negl \\
State\, \mathcal{S}_c: \quad & [X(\mathcal{A}_c)] && = && (\prec x_0, 0\succ, (inc\ inf)) \\
& [Q(\mathcal{A}_c)] && = && ((\text{HALO}\ q_0\ -), (dec\ fin)) \\
& [F(\mathcal{A}_c)] && = && ((\text{HALO}\ f_0\ +), (inc\ fin)) && \text{Persistence:} && negl \\
& && && && \text{Arrival:} && negl \\
State\, \mathcal{S}_d: \quad & [X(\mathcal{A}_d)] && = && ((\text{HALO}\ 0\ -), (inc\ inf)) \\
& [Q(\mathcal{A}_d)] && = && ((\text{HALO}\ q_0\ -), (dec\ fin)) \\
& [F(\mathcal{A}_d)] && = && ((\text{HALO}\ f_0\ +), (inc\ fin)) && \text{Persistence:} && negl \\
& && && && \text{Arrival:} && negl \\
State\, \mathcal{S}_e: \quad & [X(\mathcal{A}_e)] && = && (0, (inc\ inf)) \\
& [Q(\mathcal{A}_e)] && = && ((\text{HALO}\ q_0\ -), (dec\ fin)) \\
& [F(\mathcal{A}_e)] && = && ((\text{HALO}\ f_0\ +), (inc\ fin)) && \text{Persistence:} && 0 \\
\end{aligned}
$$

Figure 3.13
Behavior of an Infinite Flow Rate Heat Exchanger

standard behaviors alternate between states persisting for closed time points and ones lasting for open intervals of standard real duration. This implies that there is a finite, noninfinitesimal time between any two events that do not occur in the same standard state.

The time is easy to measure in exaggerated behaviors as well, because HR-QSIM's successor-arrival filtering step computes arrival times for each state. All that is required is a means of adding the times from individual states to determine the length of a whole behavioral fragment. Qualitative addition of times is defined in by the table of figure 3.14; notice that this is just the maximum operator.

The scale phase answers questions about durations by comparing the elapsed time between corresponding events. For example, consider the straightforward comparative analysis question "Does the oil exit the pipe sooner if if moves faster?" Event descriptions of $X = x_0$ and $X = 0$ specify the starting and ending states $\mathcal{S}_1$ and $\mathcal{S}_3$ in the standard

3.4. Scale Phase

	inf	fin	negl	0
inf	inf	inf	inf	inf
fin	inf	fin	fin	fin
negl	inf	fin	negl	negl
0	inf	fin	negl	0

Figure 3.14
Temporal Addition

behavior and S_a and S_e in the exaggerated one. Since $S_1 \neq S_3$ the standard oil remains in the heat exchanger for finite time. Since the arrival times of the states between S_a and S_e are all *negl*, temporal addition concludes that the oil requires negligible time to leave the heat exchanger when the flow rate is infinite. Since *negl* < *fin*, the scale phase concludes that in general, the oil will exit sooner if the flow rate is increased.

One might ask why arrival times are used rather than adding the persistence values for the relevant states. The reason that arrival values are the relevant metric is because the question is how long does it take to *reach* the state of interest. For the heat exchanger example it makes little difference whether arrival or persistence times are used, but consider the case of a projectile moving at constant, *fin* speed. How long does it take to reach *inf* from zero? There are two intervening qualitative values: (HALO 0 +) and ≺0, *inf*≻. The sum of the persistences is: 0+*fin*=*fin*, while the sum of the arrival times is *negl*+*inf*=*inf*. This latter answer is clearly the intuitive one.

Since there is still ambiguity in the distance-rate-time table even with the infinite arrival rule, some states may not have firm arrival values. In these cases, it can be impossible to determine the exact length of an exaggerated behavioral fragment, so the scale phase may not be able to answer the comparative analysis question. If one of the other states in the fragment has an *inf* arrival value, however, then one can conclude that the whole behavior will persist for *inf* time even if some states are ambiguous. Thus temporal ambiguity in individual states does not necessarily doom the scale phase.

3.4.2 Multiple Behaviors

The preceding discussion finessed one point — it assumed that there was only one standard and one exaggerated behavior. Since frequently neither of these assumptions is true, the scale phase algorithm is more complicated. For example, QSIM predicts three behaviors for the standard heat exchanger. Figure 3.12 represents the behavior in which the oil exits before reaching thermal equilibrium, but behaviors in which thermal equilibrium is reached before the oil exits and exactly when the oil exits are also possible. Although HR-QSIM predicts a unique behavior for the infinite rate heat exchanger, this is not the case for all examples.

Thus, the scale phase can't necessarilly just compare the value of a parameter from a single standard behavior to a single exaggerated behavior. Two possibilities exist: compare all exaggerated behaviors to some specific standard behavior or compare all standard behaviors pairwise with the exaggerated behaviors. The current implementation does the former — it takes advantage of the information implicit in the modeler's choice of a single behavior. For the question "What happens to output temperature if the flow rate is increased?", the choice of initial behavior is irrelevant; all three standard behaviors predict that heat will decrease a finite amount while it decreases negligibly in the exaggerated behavior.

To see how the modeler's selection of an initial standard behavior facilitates exaggeration, consider the question "What happens to output temperature when thermal conductivity, K, is increased?" HR-QSIM generates a single behavior which predicts that with $K = minf$, heat transitions to zero in $negl$ time. In other words, thermal equilibrium is reached long before the oil exits the pipe. But two of the three standard QSIM behaviors also predicted that there would be zero heat as the oil left the pipe. Unless the modeler chooses the standard behavior in which the oil exits before reaching thermal equilibrium, the scale phase would have no qualitative difference on which to base an answer. By matching against a single standard behavior, exaggeration takes advantage of the knowledge in the mind of the human who chose the initial behavior, and ambiguity is reduced.

3.5 Summary

Exaggeration solves comparative analysis problems in a manner fundamentally different from DQ analysis — by converting the comparative analysis problem into a new simulation problem and analyzing the result. The process is divided into three phases: transform, simulate, and scale. This chapter traced exaggeration's performance on the question "What happens to the output temperature of hot oil in a heat exchanger when the oil's flow rate is increased?" The transform phase constructed the model of a heat exchanger where the oil moved infinitely fast. The simulate phase (implemented as the HR-QSIM algorithm) predicted that oil in this model would leave after cooling only a negligible amount. Finally, the scale phase compared the results from the standard and hyperreal qualitative simulations and noticed that the output temperature was qualitatively higher in the exaggerated case; it then concluded that, in general, increases in velocity cause increases in output temperature.

This section concentrated on the technical details of the exaggeration algorithm, in particular how HR-QSIM works. The qualitative hyperreal representation was introduced and used to motivate changes to the QSIM algorithm. Predecessor-persistence and successor-arrival filtering were shown to be critical to hyperreal simulation in two ways: they both compute important temporal information about each qualitative state and they eliminate many inconsistent transitions, restricting the number of proposed qualitative behaviors.

The next chapter compares exaggeration to DQ analysis on many dimensions: theoretical, competence, computational performance, and explanatory quality. Unlike DQ analysis, exaggeration is shown to be unsound; it's answers are not always correct. Like DQ analysis, exaggeration is incomplete. Neither technique can solve all comparative analysis problems. Exaggeration, however, appears to solve a larger class of problems than DQ analysis; the reasons for this are discussed.

4 Analysis of Techniques

This chapter compares the techniques of DQ analysis and exaggeration along several dimensions: their theoretical foundation (section 4.2), their ability to answer comparative analysis questions correctly (section 4.3), their algorithmic complexity (section 4.4), and the quality of the explanations that they produce (section 4.5). First, however, the similarities between the techniques are discussed.

4.1 Similarities and Shared Problems

The qualitative nature of both DQ analysis and exaggeration is both the key to their power and the cause of their shared weaknesses. Several classes of questions stump both techniques; in these cases, the reason is always that the qualitative abstraction is inappropriate for the problem at hand. The cases are divided into three groups: questions that are fundamentally ambiguous, questions that result in ambiguity from qualitative arithmetic, and questions that depend on the distinction between linear and monotonic functions.

4.1.1 Ambiguous Questions

Some questions simply don't contain enough information to be answerable. For example, neither DQ analysis nor exaggeration could answer the question "What would happen to the period of oscillation, if the mass of the block was heavier and the spring was more stiff?" because there is no answer to this question as stated. The increased mass tends to increase the period, but the increased spring constant tends to decrease it. Thus the duration might increase, decrease or remain unchanged.

Neither technique answers incorrectly; they both terminate without generating an answer. It would be nice if my techniques could tell that there was no answer and complain that the question was poorly phrased, but as it is, neither exaggeration nor DQ analysis recognizes that the difficulty is in the question rather than inadequate reasoning abilities.

4.1.2 Qualitative Arithmetic is Ambiguous

Since DQ analysis and exaggeration use the same qualitative arithmetic utilized by other forms of qualitative reasoning, it should not be surprising that ambiguity causes a problem here as well.

The model of a projectile fired from a cannon in a uniform gravitational field serves to demonstrate the problems due to qualitative arithmetic. Neither technique can deduce that the time to apogee will not change if the projectile mass is increased. The culprit is inherent ambiguity of qualitative values— relative change values do not form a group under multiplication [60] and thus there are not guaranteed inverses. This affects DQ analysis as follows. Since M is increased but G remains unchanged, $F = MG$ leads to the conclusion that $F\Uparrow$. But what is the relative change value for acceleration? $F = MA$ results in ambiguity because there is no unique value for $\Uparrow$ divided by $\Uparrow$. Exaggeration faces the same problem: if mass is infinite, then force must be also. But since there is no unique value for *inf* divided by *inf*, acceleration could be *negl*, *fin*, or *inf*. This problem affects all qualitative reasoning systems; qualitative simulation programs have the same problem as those for comparative analysis.

Another example, the oscillating spring / block clearly shows the parallel. Although both techniques deduce that increasing mass will increase the time taken from an initial extreme until the first transition ($X = 0$) is reached, neither technique can deduce that the whole period will increase in length (without explicit equations for energy conservation in the model). Because of the qualitative arithmetic, DQ analysis is unable to show that $X\|_2$, i.e., that X sweeps out the same distance when the mass is increased. Because of this, X is not known to be a covering perspective so the derivative and duration theorems can not be used. Thus there is no way to determine the RC value for the second quarter of the period. Exaggeration displays the same problem of ambiguity in the temporal filtering algorithms. With an infinite mass, acceleration is negligible and velocity is transitioning from a negligible value towards zero. Since the qualitative value of velocity has *negl* width and the distance to the qualitative value is also *negl*, neither predecessor-persistence nor successor-arrival filtering can say whether the transition will take *negl*, *fin*, or (the correct answer) *inf* time.

This problem is directly analogous to QSIM's prediction of spurious behaviors [38]. Given a Hooke's law description of the spring/block, QSIM produces many possible behaviors in addition to the correct description of stable oscillation. Furthermore, both the DQ problem and exaggeration's impotence can be alleviated in the same way that Kuipers caused QSIM to disregard behaviors other than stable oscillation—by augmenting the structural description with equations describing conservation of energy. DQ analysis, for example, can deduce that since

4.1. Similarities and Shared Problems

potential energy is equal to force times distance, increasing the block's mass leaves total energy unchanged. This allows it to recognize X as a covering perspective and deduce that the duration increases for each of the period's four transition intervals. Similarly, exaggeration can perform persistence and arrival filtering on the additional parameters to conclude that it takes *inf* time for the block to reach it's extreme position.

The problem of ambiguous qualitative arithmetic is an important area for future work. One approach is inspired by the success of the manual inclusion of redundant (conservation) equations; perhaps it would be appropriate for programs to perform some symbolic algebraic manipulation before generating qualitative solutions [74]. Struss [60] has shown that care must be exercised in this activity, since small changes in the form of qualitative equations frequently result in radical changes to their solutions. Dormoy and Raiman [18] recently demonstrated the qualitative resolution rule, a type of algebraic manipulation that is solution preserving. While it cannot eliminate all problems with ambiguity, it would help with the projectile problem above. Incorporation of a limited algebraic reasoner into qualitative reasoning systems seems very promising.

4.1.3 Linearity is not Represented

A second problem faced by both DQ analysis and exaggeration is the insensitivity of qualitative techniques to the difference between a linear function and one which is simply monotonic. For example, given the Hooke's law description of an oscillating spring and block on a frictionless, horizontal surface $(F = -KX)$, neither technique can answer the question "What happens to the period of oscillation if the amplitude is increased?"

In fact, the answer is that the period does not change, but exaggeration can not predict this because of ambiguity in the successor-arrival and predecessor-persistence filters. The transform phase constructs an initial state with infinite displacement, and constraint propagation concludes that force and acceleration must also be infinite. The infinite arrival rule predicts that velocity will transition to infinity in negligible time, but then ambiguity sets in. With $V = inf$, the question is how long will it take X to move from inf to zero? Unfortunately, the distance-rate-time table is ambiguous and the infinite-distance arrival rule (proposition 17) does not apply since X is moving from infinity rather than to infinity. It could take *negl*, *fin*, or *inf* time for X to transition and HR-QSIM cannot determine which.

DQ analysis cannot solve the question either, apparently for a very different reason: no useful perspective,noneperspective exists to enable the duration rule. There is no system parameter P such that $V\|_{(0,1)}^{P}$. Clearly X won't work as a perspective, since it doesn't sweep out the same range in the two cases. In fact, it is easy to prove that no artificial perspective could satisfy the equation.

Proposition 19 *Given the definition of V as specified above for the spring/block example with $X\Uparrow_0$, let $t_1 = T(\gamma_1)$ and $\hat{t}_1 = \widehat{T}(\gamma_1)$. There are no continuous, real valued, functions $P, \widehat{P}$ such that*

$$\begin{aligned}
P(0) &= \widehat{P}(0) = p_0 \wedge \\
P(t_1) &= \widehat{P}(\hat{t}_1) = p_1 \wedge \\
\widehat{V}(\widehat{P}^{-1}(p)) &= V(P^{-1}(p)) \; \forall p \in (p_0, p_1)
\end{aligned}$$

Proof: Since $X\Uparrow_0$, initial potential energy is higher in the perturbed system, so kinetic energy is greater at γ_1. This means that $V\Uparrow_1$, i.e.,

$$\widehat{V}(\hat{t}_1) = \hat{v}_1 > v_1 = V(t_1)$$

Because $\widehat{V}$ and V are continuous

$$\lim_{t \to \hat{t}_1} \widehat{V}(t) = \hat{v}_1$$

and

$$\lim_{t \to t_1} V(t) = v_1$$

Similarly,

$$\lim_{p \to \hat{p}_1} \widehat{P^{-1}}(p) = \hat{p}_1$$

and

$$\lim_{p \to p_1} P^{-1}(p) = p_1$$

Thus
$$\lim_{p \to \hat{p}_1} (\widehat{V}(\widehat{P^{-1}}(p)) - V(P^{-1}(p))) = \widehat{v_1} - v_1 \neq 0$$
So there exists some $q \in (p_0, p_1)$ such that
$$\widehat{V}(\widehat{P}^{-1}(q)) = V(P^{-1}(q))$$
□

Thus there is no function, P, that can act as a perspective such that $V\|_{(0,1)}^P$. This really shouldn't be very surprising. After all, the block really does move faster. The only reason that the period is unchanged is that the increased velocity is exactly counterbalanced by the increased distance the block must travel. It would be foolish to try and claim the velocity doesn't increase when it does. Instead, an intuitive explanation should account for the balance of the change in velocity and distance.

This type of explanation is outside the realm of current theories of qualitative physics because it depends on the fact that Hooke's law is a linear equation. Nonlinear oscillators, like pendulums, *do* change their period when amplitude is changed. Because qualitative techniques do not distinguish between linear and nonlinear, yet monotonic, functions, they are incapable of solving questions that depend on those distinctions. Future work might investigate the possibility of explicit reasoning about linear equations, and the related issue of symmetry.

4.2 Theoretical Difference

This section considers several questions relating to the theoretical difference between exaggeration and DQ analysis. What are the techniques doing? Why do they perform differently? Can either technique substitute for the other if augmented with additional knowledge or assumptions? The short answers are that the two techniques are fundamentally different. While each technique can be augmented to simulate the other, the assumptions required are not always realistic.

4.2.1 Predicting Partial Derivatives

Since the relative change notation expresses how a parameter changes given an initial perturbation, it is natural to ask about its relationship to the standard mathematical tools for expressing relative change: partial derivatives. In the following proposition it is handy to think of parameter C as the cause, and E as an effect.

Proposition 20 *If $C\Uparrow_0$ and all other independent and boundary condition parameters have an RC value of $\|_0$ and $E\Downarrow_0$ then*

$$\frac{\partial E}{\partial C} < 0$$

at time zero.

This statement can be extended to any transition, γ_i, by normalizing with respect to time. While the relationship between RC values and partial derivative is straightforward for values at transition points, the connection is more subtle for interval RC values because of the presence of perspectives.

Exaggeration Requires Monotonicity Although both techniques try to find the sign of the partial derivative of one parameter with respect to another, they do it in different ways. DQ analysis computes the partial derivative's sign directly, while exaggeration approximates the partial derivative by evaluating the equation at an asymptote and returning the slope of a straight line though this limiting value and the original point.

To understand these points, it is useful to consider examples that are even simpler than the heat exchanger. The question of partial derivatives is complicated by the fact that the heat exchanger parameters are defined with differential equations and change over time. Comparative analysis seeks the partial derivative of the *solution* of the differential equation model. By considering simple algebraic equations instead of differential equations, the problem of solving the equations is eliminated and the fundamental difference between DQ analysis and exaggeration illuminated.

For example, consider the equation:

$$Y = 5 + \frac{1}{X}$$

A simple comparative analysis question would be "What happens to Y if X is increased?" In other words, what is the sign of $\frac{\partial Y}{\partial X}$? DQ analysis solves this by propagating the perturbation through the equation: if $X\Uparrow$

4.2. Theoretical Difference

then $\frac{1}{X}\Downarrow$. Since $5\|$, DQ analysis concludes that $Y\Downarrow$. Exaggeration, on the other hand, evaluates the equation to find Y's value when X is inf. Because $\frac{1}{X} = negl$, this asymptotic value for Y is lower than its current value. The scale phase concludes that the qualitative partial derivative is $\Downarrow$.

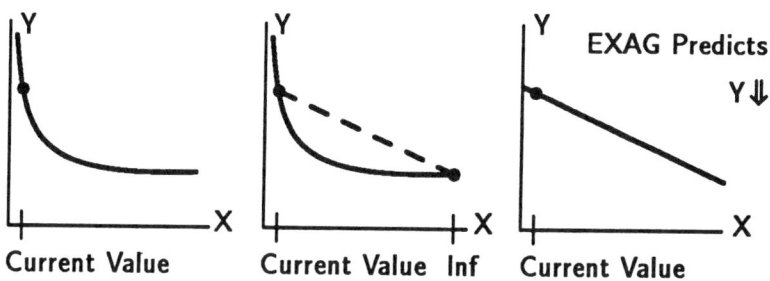

Figure 4.1
Exaggeration Approximates a Curve with a Line through an Asymptote

Since the scale phase can be thought of as approximating the partial derivative by drawing the slope of a straight line between the current and asymptotic values (figure 4.1), it might appear that exaggeration would produce sound answers only for linear systems. However, since comparative analysis only requires the sign of the partial derivative, exaggeration only requires that a system respond monotonically to the perturbation, not linearly.

4.2.2 Predicting Asymptotes

As the previous section considered what assumptions were necessary to guarantee that exaggeration correctly predict qualitative partial derivatives, it is natural to ask what knowledge must be added to DQ analysis to achieve exaggeration's ability to predict asymptotic values. Consider the following two equations:

$$Y = 5 + \frac{1}{X}$$
$$Y = 8 + \frac{1}{X}$$

As X tends towards inf, Y takes on different values in these two equations, yet the partial derivative (and hence the relative change value predicted by DQ analysis) is the same. Given a quantitative representation, the assumption of linearity would allow one to predict Y's value for any value of X. However, a linearity assumption is not strong enough for prediction of asymptotic values given a qualitative representation. The relative change value predicted by DQ analysis can accurately predict an asymptotic value only when the function is constant. This case is so trivial, it is unlikely to be useful.

This analysis shows the theoretical relationship between the two techniques, yet the question remains: "For any given problem, which technique will work better?" The next section discusses this issue.

4.3 Competence Difference

There are several possible meanings to the question "Which technique works better?" Here I consider competence: "When does each technique work?" An ideal answer would be a characterization of the sets of comparative analysis questions that each technique correctly solves. Although this discussion is not that precise, it does illuminate the reasons for differences in competence. Neither technique is strictly stronger — each has advantages that enables it to out perform the other on a subclass of problems. The discussion starts with questions that stump exaggeration and then consideres the weaknesses of DQ analysis.

4.3.1 Weaknesses of Exaggeration

The first difference in competence was introduced in the previous section: nonmonotonicity. The following simple algebraic example shows exaggeration's weakness with nonmonotonic systems.

$$Y = X + \frac{1}{X}$$

DQ analysis is unable to answer the question "What happens to Y if X is increased?" because of ambiguity: Since $X\Uparrow$ and $\frac{1}{X}\Downarrow$, the sum is indeterminate. This is as it should be; the answer depends on the original quantitative value of X and is thus outside qualitative reasoning.

Exaggeration, however, willingly supplies an answer. If $X = inf$ then $\frac{1}{X} = negl$ so $Y = inf$, thus by approximating the curve with a straight line, the scale phase would conclude that increasing X increases Y (figure

4.3. Competence Difference

4.2a) and hence decreasing X decreases Y. But if the transform phase exaggerated X to an infinitesimal value, then $\frac{1}{X}$ would equal *inf* so Y would equal *inf*. This would suggest the opposite: that increasing X decreases Y. The results are inconsistent; whichever transformation exaggeration makes will result in an incorrect answer for some initial value of X.

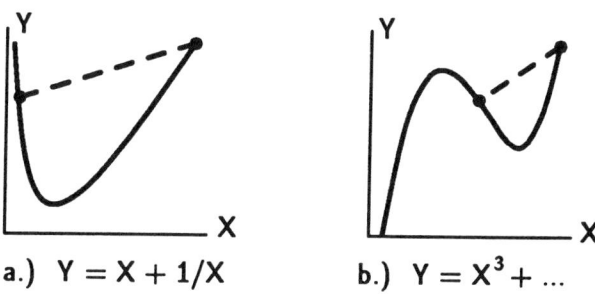

a.) $Y = X + 1/X$ b.) $Y = X^3 + ...$

Figure 4.2
Nonmonotonic Systems can Fool Exaggeration

While it is easy to check the monotonicity of an algebraic equation by finding the roots of its derivative, there is no easy way to ensure monotonicity of the *solution* of an arbitrary system of differential equations. The trick of exaggerating in both directions suffices to detect simple types of nonmonotonicity with one inflection point, but fails to detect nonmonotonic functions like cubic equations (figure 4.2b). Perhaps the only way to verify exaggeration's soundness would be to step out of qualitative reasoning and solve the differential equations using standard algebraic techniques. For linear equations, a closed form solution would be easily obtainable. If the equations were nonlinear, Sacks' PLR program [52, 53] could be used to generate and solve a piecewise linear approximation. Although neither of these techniques generates explanations, they could be used to check monotonicity and thus validate exaggeration's predictions.

4.3.2 Weaknesses of DQ Analysis

While DQ analysis, unlike exaggeration, is guaranteed to answer CA questions correctly, it is common for DQ analysis to produce no answer at all. Exaggeration can correctly solve many problems that are too difficult for DQ analysis. An example of a projectile fired from a cannon illustrates this point. Given an increase in muzzle velocity, $V\Uparrow_0$, as a perturbation, DQ analysis predicts that apogee will occur later, but is unable to predict that the projectile will rise higher or take longer to fall back to the ground. If energy conservation equations are added explicitly, then DQ analysis reaches the correct conclusion. However, exaggeration gets the right answer to all these questions without requiring energy conservation equations.

If one considers a more realistic projectile model in which gravity diminishes with increasing altitude, then DQ analysis fails to conclude any of the three results — even with energy conservation equations. Exaggeration, on the other hand, correctly answers all three.

Why does DQ analysis perform so poorly? The problem appears to be that the DQ analysis rules match on the syntax of the system's differential equation model. For example, one common rule applies when a parameter's derivative is a linear function of the parameter. Since the rule only has access to the model's syntactic description, it might fire if the model unified with the patterns (D/DT ?x ?v) and (MULT ?x ?k ?v). But what if the model was more indirect and included the two equations $V = KU$ and $U = KX$ instead of $V = KX$? If K was a positive constant, the two formulations would be equivalent, but the system would not know it. Since there are an infinite number of ways to write equivalent models, a finite set of rules cannot recognize them all without help. If all models were expressed as sets of first order linear equations, then it might be possible for an algebraic manipulator to translate them into canonical form. But since nonlinear models are allowed and can contain arbitrary monotonic function constraints, this is not obviously feasible.

Exaggeration is less sensitive to model differences since it does not try to differentiate the equations, only evaluate them. For the sets of differential equations that are used to model physical systems evaluation means qualitative simulation; the result is a time behavior that satisfies the differential equation. When two sets of differential equations evaluate (simulate) to the same values (time behaviors), exaggeration considers them equivalent. Thus exaggeration reaches answers more frequently because simulating a differential equation model is easier than directly computing the partial derivatives of its solution.

4.3. Competence Difference

The following example demonstrates a different form of brittleness in DQ analysis which is also caused by a lack of algebraic reasoning. Imagine two containers, each initially filled to the same level with liquid. Suppose that a pump moves liquid from container B to A, but that the wall between the containers is permiable. If there is a pressure gradient from A to B, then liquid will seep backwards. The system can be modeled with seven parameters, the fluid level in the containers L_a and L_b, the difference in height[1] H, the rate of pumped and seeping flow F_p and F_s, net flow F_n and the permiability of the wall separating the containers P, obeying the following constraints:

$$L_b = \text{MINUS}(L_a) \qquad (4.1)$$

$$L_a = \text{ADD}(L_b, H) \qquad (4.2)$$

$$F_s = \text{MULT}(H, P) F_n = \text{ADD}(F_p, F_s) \qquad (4.3)$$

$$F_n = \tfrac{d}{dt} L_a \qquad (4.4)$$

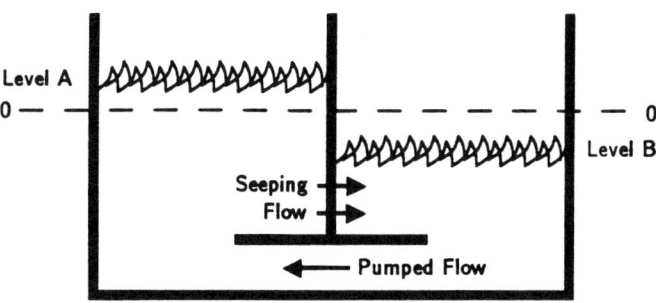

Figure 4.3
Equilibrium State for Pumped Containers

Given this model, QSIM quickly determines that the height difference between the two containers will rise until an equilibrium value is reached in which there is no net flow (figure 4.3). Both DQ analysis and

---
[1] Height difference is also used to represent difference in pressure.

exaggeration correctly solve the comparative analysis question "What happens to the height difference if the rate of pumped flow is greater?" DQ analysis uses the following line of reasoning:

> Since there is a greater pumped flow, the rate of seepage must be greater at equilibrium. This means that the height (pressure) difference must be greater.

This explanation is simple and to the point. Unfortunately, DQ analysis (unlike exaggeration) does not realize that L_a is higher at equilibrium even though this is a simple algebraic consequence of a greater height. This inadequacy would not be solved by preprocessing the differential equation model into canonical form. Postprocessing the output of DQ analysis, however, might increase coverage. This is an interesting avenue for future research.

As explained in the section above, different types of ambiguity are the cause for the incompleteness of DQ analysis. Yet DQ analysis handles ambiguity differently from other forms of qualitative reasoning. For example, when QSIM is faced with ambiguity about a parameter's value, it branches, spawning perhaps three new behaviors: one with the parameter equal to a landmark value, one greater and one less. QSIM can do this because the nature of inequality guarantees that either $A < B$, $A = B$, or $A > B$. While this is true for RC values at transition points, it is not true for RC values over intervals.

Proposition 21 Non–Exhaustivity
Given two parameters, V and P, such that P is a covering perspective over an interval (γ_i, γ_{i+1}), it is not necessarily the case that one of $V\Uparrow^P_{(i,i+1)}$, $V\|^P_{(i,i+1)}$, or $V\Downarrow^P_{(i,i+1)}$ holds.

Proof: Appendix B provides an example which proves this statement □

Thus unlike qualitative simulators, DQ analysis can not branch when faced with uncertainty, it simply acts mute.

4.4 Performance Difference

This section considers the worst case computational complexity of the two comparative analysis techniques. The quick answer is that asymptotically DQ analysis is considerably more efficient than exaggeration:

4.4. Performance Difference

polynomial rather than exponential in the length of simulation time. However, DQ analysis requires a qualitative behavior as input and computing this is exponential in the worst case. In practice, exaggeration runs a bit more quickly than DQ analysis.

4.4.1 DQ Analysis is Polynomial

Since DQ analysis is implemented as a forward chaining rule system based on a propositional database, two kinds of operations are suggested as possible computational metrics: the number of database matches and the number of actual rule firings. There are two reasons why the number of database matches is the best metric. Since no rule can fire before being matched to the database, the number of matches is a more conservative metric and thus more appropriate as a worst case measurement. Secondly, informal metering of the ARK substrate indicates that the vast majority of compute time is actually spent performing the matches.

Unlike many forward chaining systems, one can show that DQ analysis has a tight bound on the number of entries that can be stored in the database. This in turn limits the number of matches that can be performed before the rule system reaches quiescence.

Each database entry is one of a constant number of types. The 'relative change over an interval' type is the most important from the perspective of this analysis because it has the greatest number of independent slots and thus spawns the greatest potential number of entries. Since this type's pattern is instantiated by two parameter slots (one for the parameter being compared and one for the perspective) and one time slot, there are $\Theta(TP^2)$ entries in the database where P is the number of parameters in the system and T is the temporal length of the behavior.

Every time that a new entry is made to the database, it is matched against every rule to see if it enables one to fire. Assuming R rules and E entries, the number of matches is greater than $\Theta(RE)$ because some entries can be matched against some rules in more than one way. For example, it is very common for the conjunctive antecedent of a rule to contain two patterns of the same type, as shown in figure 4.4.

If there were E database entries with this 'relative change over an interval' type, then this rule might be satisfied $\Theta(E^2)$ ways. Since the set of rules is fixed, there exists a finite bound, a, on the maximum

```
(⇒ (AND (RC ?v (?start ?middle) ?c (P- ?x))
        (RC ?v (?middle ?end) ?c (P- ?x)))
   (RC ?v (?start ?end) ?c (P- ?x))
   stupid-rule)
```

Figure 4.4
A Sample Rule

number of conjuncts in a rule antecedent.[2] Thus the total number of database matches is $\Theta(RE^a)$ or equivalently $\Theta(RT^a P^{2a})$.

Although this is a worst case analysis, the average case complexity is probably similar. For systems of seven parameters, with behaviors that contain ten time points or intervals, running in the current base of eighty rules, it takes about three minutes to reach quiescence.

Note that DQ analysis requires a qualitative behavior as input. Since generating such a behavior is exponential in the worst case [38], it is a bit unfair to label DQ analysis polynomial. Experience with the current implementation (which usess QSIM to produce behaviors) shows that the worst case is seldom realized with simple examples; simulating a system rarely takes over a minute.

4.4.2 Exaggeration is Exponential

Let P denote the number of parameters in the system, let C be the number of constraints, and T the length of time before the event of interest. The transform phase is fast, $\Theta(P)$ since the most expensive operation is the reformulation of each parameter's quantity space.

As a first step in the complexity analysis of the simulate phase, consider the time required for HR-QSIM to generate the successors of a qualitative state. The analysis is very similar to that of QSIM [38, page 312]. Transition tables generate possible values in $\Theta(P)$ time. The most expensive constraint filter is the check of corresponding values which grow over time resulting in a complexity of $\Theta(PT)$ time. Waltz filtering requires $\Theta(C)$ time. Unfortunately, when the parameter values are combined into global interpretations, $\Theta(2^P)$ interpretations are possible in the worst case. In practice, the number of interpretations

---
[2] For the current rule set $a \approx 6$.

is much smaller, between three and one, decreasing as the number of constraints rises. Predecessor-persistence and successor-arrival filtering require $\Theta(P)$ time for each interpretation.

Thus, on average HR-QSIM, like QSIM before it, produces each successor state in linear time. While it is possible to construct pathological cases where each state has an exponential number of successors, these seem quite rare. Even with the common case of bounded branching, however, the situation is far from rosy. Since HR-QSIM generates a tree of states in breadth first fashion, the number of states produced is exponential in T, the maximum time considered. In fact, the situation is effectively worse for HR-QSIM than it is for QSIM. Because parameters pass through infinitesimal halos on their way from a landmark to a finite interval, more qualitative states are needed to represent the 'same' behavior. This means that T is almost twice as large for a HR-QSIM behavior as for an analogous QSIM behavior.

The scale phase is also worst-case exponential in T because it needs to compare each behavior against the original QSIM behavior. The number of HR-QSIM behaviors is equal to the number of leaves on the state tree which is exponential in the depth, T, of the tree. In practice, the constant factor is so much lower for the scale phase than the simulate phase, that its speed is not an issue.

The preceding analysis is worst case. For many problems, HR-QSIM produces a single unbranching behavior and runs in less than a minute. Out of the more than fifty comparative analysis problems attempted, only three had truly intractable branching (appendix F). With these problems additional heuristics or manual search control would have been necessary for exaggeration to reach an answer.

4.5 Explanation Difference

A final question applies to those comparative analysis problems that are answered by both techniques. Which of the resulting explanations is better? Since comparative analysis is distinguished from sensitivity analysis by its ability to generate explanations, this is an important question to answer. Unfortunately, the multitude of factors affecting the perceived quality of an explanation make this difficult question as well. I start by addressing criteria for a good explanation.

4.5.1 What Makes a Good Explanation?

While psychological studies are probably the best way to measure the quality of explanations, such studies are beyond the scope of this book. Instead, I present abstract desiderata that explanations should meet. One factor not included is the quality of the natural language text, since I am concerned with the nature of the underlying argument, not the way in which that argument is presented. In fact, DQ analysis has only a rudimentary algorithm for transforming proof trees into English text, while no such algorithm has been implemented for exaggeration. It goes without saying that any argument is improved by good diction, but the issues involved are unrelated to those of this book.

- The most obvious criterion is that the explanation should answer the question and do so correctly. Section 4.3 showed that DQ analysis meets this requirement, but exaggeration does not.

- The explanation should be grounded in information already known by the listener. Unless this criterion is met, the listener cannot graft the explanation into his previous understanding and will remain confused. Both DQ analysis and exaggeration meet this requirement by only using information that is made explicit in the problem specification. Note that I have not addressed the major question of student modeling. The problem of gauging what a person knows and choosing an understandable and appropriate model is a topic for future research.

- The explanation should not contain extraneous information that might confuse or distract the listener. DQ analysis certainly satisfies this requirement—the constraint propagator maintains a dependency structure showing which rules led to any conclusion and exactly what facts were involved. A differential qualitative explanation is simply a reformatted version of the dependency tree.

  At one level exaggerated explanations meet this requirement, but at another level the current implementation is deficient. The distinction is one of detail in the explanation. If one assumes that the explanation does not need to explain *why* the exaggerated system has the behavior predicted by HR-QSIM, then no irrelevant facts are introduced. The conclusion follows directly from an observation of a difference in the standard and hyperreal behaviors.

4.5. Explanation Difference

However, if one assumes that the explanation should justify the hyperreal behavior, then irrelevancies occur. The problem is the fundamental way that QSIM is structured. Rather than deducing causal connections between parametric values, QSIM (and HR-QSIM) generate the space of all possible behaviors and then discard the inconsistent ones. Although the strategy results in an elegant and (on average) speedy algorithm, there is no way to justify a behavior other than to say that the alternatives were inconsistent. As a result there is no way to isolate the facts that underlie a parameter's hyperreal value. Fortunately, this limitation is not basic to the idea of exaggeration, only to this implementation of the simulate phase. If any of the other qualitative simulators [21, 11, 69] had been used as a basis for the simulate phase, this problem would not apply.

- The explanation should not require mathematical sophistication. While mathematical arguments will quickly convince those who appreciate them, people unfamiliar with mathematical concepts and notation will likely get lost. Both DQ analysis and exaggeration produce explanations that meet this goal.

- The explanation should be short. Long and complicated arguments are by definition more difficult to understand. The problem is to be precise about measuring the length of an explanation. The next section argues that for a class of comparative analysis problems, exaggeration generates explanations that are simpler than those produced by DQ analysis.

- The explanation should say familiar things in familiar ways. If obvious points are couched in unfamiliar terms, then recognition and comprehension take longer. Section 4.5.3 explains why both DQ analysis and exaggeration sometimes generate unnatural explanations.

It is interesting to note that the popular learning technique, explanation based generalization (EBG) [41, 16], uses the word 'explanation' in the same sense that I do. The fact that EBG requires the first three of my criteria to generalize successfully lends extra weight to the desiderata. To support this argument I implemented an EBG algorithm [34] that correctly generalizes the explanations produced by DQ analysis (section 2.3).

4.5.2 Exaggeration can Produce Simpler Answers

In some cases DQ analysis and exaggeration produce similar explanations, but there are also cases when the explanations are very different. The oscillating spring / block is an example of a system on which the two perform similarly. Given a question about the relative change of period caused by an increase in mass, DQ analysis deduces that force is the same, so acceleration is smaller, so velocity is smaller, so the time is longer. Exaggeration needs a similar line of reasoning to justify the fact that a block with infinite mass has infinite period: force is finite, so acceleration is infinitesimal, so velocity is infinitesimal, and so on.

More interesting are the explanations that are not parallel. A good example is the question "What happens to output temperature when hot oil passes more quickly through a heat exchanger?" A DQ explanation needs to follow through the details of the constraint model of heat flow, but an exaggerated explanation can disregard the details of heat flow because it has negligible effect when the oil moves infinitely fast. Consider the following possible heat exchangers (not all implemented):

- Hot oil flows through a bath of coolant held at constant temperature.

- Hot oil flows through a bath of coolant that gradually warms.

- Hot oil flows down a pipe in one direction while warming coolant flows through a concentric pipe in the other direction.

- Hot oil and coolant flow in same direction through concentric pipes.

- Any of the above models with thermal conductivity changing as a function of temperature difference.

- Any of the above models complicated by modeling the thermal mass of the pipe wall. This causes two heat flows: from the oil to the pipe wall then from the wall to the coolant.

In fact DQ analysis can only answer the comparative analysis question on the first (and simplest) heat exchanger model, but if it could reason

4.5. Explanation Difference

about the others its answers would get more and more complicated. The exaggerated answer, on the other hand, could remain the same for each of these models. The details of the heat flow process are irrelevant since the flow rate is only finite and the oil is moving infinitely fast. In these cases the exaggerated explanation is simpler because it abstracts irrelevant detail from the heat flow process.

Although the answer is simpler, the simulate phase of exaggeration makes no simplifying assumptions and in fact performs more work on the more complex models. Getting computer problem solvers to autonomously refine their models with simplifying assumptions is an important subject for future research.

4.5.3 Unnatural Explanations

Both DQ analysis and exaggeration sometimes generate correct, yet unnatural explanations. The underlying cause of the awkwardness is the expression of a familiar idea in an unfamiliar way.

For example take the question "What happens to the output temperature of the hot oil if it moves more rapidly through the heat exchanger?" Since the oil is cooling as it moves through the exchanger, one would like the answer expressed "The oil will cool less" rather than "It will exit hotter." Unfortunately, neither DQ analysis nor exaggeration makes commitment to a strong process ontology [21] that would facilitate this distinction.

A second example of a correct yet cognitively dissonant explanation concerns the use of perspectives in DQ analysis. Many times a problem can be solved using one of several perspectives and to the program they all look alike. As a result, the explanation might be parameterized in terms of, say, force rather than position. Although the argument would be right, it would be unfamiliar. The problem is not new [9], but it won't go away without careful heuristics explaining common ways of viewing the world.

A third example of awkwardness applies only to exaggeration. The idea behind exaggeration is to transform a small perturbation into a change that is large enough to make the overall influence obvious. In this book, I discuss transformations to infinite and infinitesimal values because these values have qualitatively different behavior that can be deduced abstractly. Since people live in the world and remember past observations, they don't always need to use such extreme examples. Often they can simply remember an exaggerated system that is adequate for the scale phase without performing simulation. In other words a perfectly valid (and natural) exaggerated explanation of the increased mass oscillator example might be:

> What happens to the period of oscillation if you increase the mass of the block? Well, Uncle Fred had an oscillator like this with a wicked big mass and it sure did have a long period. Thus, I bet an increase in mass increases period.

A related example emphasizes this problem. Imagine a projectile fired upwards at some velocity. What happens to the projectile's flight time if initial velocity is decreased? Exaggeration solves this problem correctly with the following argument:

> If the initial velocity was negligible, then the projectile would stop climbing after a negligible time since gravity causes a finite deceleration. In this time, the projectile would have climbed only a negligible distance, so the fall time will also be negligible. Thus a negligible velocity results in negligible flight time so decreasing velocity decreases flight time.

While this explanation is correct, it is rather unnatural. A much simpler explanation is the following:

> If the initial velocity was zero, the projectile wouldn't go anywhere. In other words, the flight time would be zero. Thus decreasing initial velocity decreases flight time.

The current theory of exaggeration specifies transforming to a positive infinitesimal rather than zero because it is safer. Many systems become discontinuous when a parameter goes to zero and this give unreliable answers.[3] In this example, a transform value of zero is safe and actually preferable to the value of *negl*. However, the general problem of determining the most natural explanation is a difficult one.

---

[3] For example, try exaggerating the spring constant to zero in the oscillating spring / block example, or oil velocity to zero in the heat exchanger system.

4.6 Combining the Techniques

Since the strengths of DQ analysis and exaggeration are complementary, it is natural to consider combining them. The advantage of DQ analysis is the guarantee that when it answers a question, the explanation is correct. Exaggeration, on the other hand, can generate incorrect answers for systems in which the perturbation causes nonmonotonic changes in parameter values. There appears to be no general, qualitative method of ensuring that a system reacts monotonically.

On the other hand, exaggeration appears to solve many more comparative analysis problems than does DQ analysis. Both techniques solve some problems that stump the other, but exaggeration has the upper hand. By combining the techniques, one could create a high level architecture more effective than either technique alone. A comparative analysis problem should first be subjected to DQ analysis. If that works, then a sound answer is guaranteed. If DQ analysis fails, then apply exaggeration. Now check exaggeration's predictions with all of the relative change values that DQ analysis is able to deduce. If they all agree, the chances are good that nonmonotonic behavior is absent. Finally, exaggerate the perturbation in the opposite direction and check that the resulting predictions are the opposite of the first transformation. Although there will still be pathological cases, these precautions would maximize the heuristic power of the exaggeration method.

5 Related Work

Despite its importance, little previous attention has been devoted to the questions of comparative analysis by artificial intelligence researchers. This chapter starts by discussing the related engineering field of sensitivity analysis, and then proceeds to summarize previous AI research of interest. Alternate temporal representations are mentioned first because they are relevant to both the DQ and exaggeration approaches. Next, de Kleer's work on IQ analysis and Forbus' approach to DQ analysis are presented. The chapter next considers AI work related to exaggeration: Raiman's FOG, Kuiper's time scale abstraction, and Davis' order of magnitude solution of qualitative differential equations.

5.1 Sensitivity Analysis

Sensitivity analysis is a common engineering technique for calculating the effect on system performance due to variations in system parameters. Comparative analysis is a qualitative version of sensitivity analysis. The sensitivity of a quantity Y to perturbations in a parameter X is defined [2] as the product:

$$\frac{\partial Y}{\partial X} \frac{X}{Y}$$

Because of its important application to design, considerable work has been done on efficient methods for calculating sensitivities. Approaches include numerical and symbolic differentiation, construction of an incremental network, and analysis of an adjoint network [2].

Compared to either DQ analysis or exaggeration, these methods have a major advantage—they generate a quantitative value for sensitivity. But sensitivity analysis has two limitations. Sensitivity analysis requires an explicit equation for all quantities of interest. Thus sensitivity analysis could not answer the spring / block problem until it was provided with a formula for period of oscillation. For linear systems like the spring / block, these equations could be derived automatically. For nonlinear systems, no general soultion technique exists. One could introduce piecewise linear approximations as suggested by Sacks [52, 53], but there is no way to ensure that the reulting equations are valid.

A more important limitation of sensitivity analysis, however, is the fact that it does not generate an explanation; all it provides is the answer.

For many purposes this is acceptable, but not for comparative analysis.

The technique of comparative statics [54, 33], long used in economics to compare two different equilibrium behaviors, suffers from the same limitation. It requires an explicit formula for the partial derivative in question.

5.2 Williams' Temporal Representation

QSIM [38] is a simple, easy to use simulator that has significantly sped the implementation of both exaggeration and DQ analysis. However, QSIM has defects; its weak temporal representation is a major problem that affects my comparative analysis techniques.

As explained by Hayes in [31], systems that represent behaviors as a sequence of states force a total ordering on transitions. Because qualitative reasoning is often unable to determine an unambiguous order of transitions, the behavior must branch to consider multiple possibilities. If events interact, the various branches often have interesting qualitative differences. But frequently, the alternate behaviors are equivalent and just complicate reasoning and consume processing resources.

To combat this problem, Williams has implemented a qualitative simulator based on history generation [72]. Just as standard qualitative simulators using Williams' temporal representation would improve on QSIM, exaggeration's simulate phase would produce fewer extraneous behaviors if it used the representation. Although this would not increase the competence of the overall exaggeration algorithm, it would simplify interpretation performed by the scale phase and might increase overall speed. The underlying techniques of predecessor-persistence and successor-arrival filtering would still be applicable.

Similarly, a DQ analysis implementation that used Williams' concise episode representation would have several advantages over CA. Williams is building such a system for use in automated design [71].

- The propositions of section 2.2 would still be true, and could be encoded more easily. CA requires explicit rules for composing durations over intervals (e.g., if DURATION$\Uparrow_{(0,1)}$ and DURATION$\Uparrow_{(1,2)}$ then DURATION$\Uparrow_{(0,2)}$). These computationally expensive rules would be subsumed by the temporal constraint propagator.

- The search for topologically distinct behaviors (section 2.5) would be simplified because the space would be smaller. By eliminating irrelevant order distinctions, the number of different behaviors would be smaller. Only if it was qualitatively interesting would there be any need to consider a behavior in which two parameters reach transitions simultaneously.

5.3 de Kleer's IQ Analysis

de Kleer's theory of incremental qualitative (IQ) analysis [9] is the predecessor of DQ analysis and marks the start of artificial intelligence work in comparative analysis. The overall goal de Kleer was trying so solve was the recognition and explanation of electronic circuit function given a schematic. The resulting program, QUAL, worked in two phases. First, the circuit was simulated to determine its qualitative behavior. Then the behavior is parsed using a grammar for common circuit functions. QUAL works successfully on hundreds of examples.

de Kleer calls QUAL's first phase causal analysis:

> Causal analysis takes a description of the circuit's topology as an input and produces a qualitative description of the circuits incremental behavior as an output ([9, page 20]).

Causal analysis is halfway between the notion of qualitative simulation and that of comparative analysis. The interesting behavior of the circuits that de Kleer investigated is not at steady state, rather it is the perturbations from equilibrium that are interesting:

> Causal analysis produces a causal argument which is a qualitative description of how the circuit equilibrates — how it responds to perturbations from it equilibrium state ([9, page 50]).

Causal analysis is implemented with a technique called IQ analysis. IQ analysis uses the same ⇑ ⇓ notation of DQ analysis, but these values refer to the values of parameter derivatives, not to the difference between parameter values in alternate worlds. In other words, IQ analysis is concerned with the evolution of a single behavior considered as a pattern of perturbations to steady state values, rather than the comparison of two alternate behaviors. As a result, IQ analysis has no explicit notion of time. When the IQ value for a parameter changes, its old value is lost. This means that IQ analysis cannot answer questions that would be easy for DQ analysis. For example, "If the perturbation to V was greater, would it take longer to reach equilibrium?"

IQ analysis is thus designed to solve a specific class of simulation problems rather than answer comparative analysis questions. However, IQ analysis inspired Forbus to consider DQ analysis, the first work on comparative analysis per se.

5.4 Forbus' DQ Analysis

In his work on qualitative process (QP) theory, Forbus introduced differential qualitative analysis [21, pages 159-161] and contrasted it with de Kleer's IQ analysis. However, Forbus attempted no implementation and his formalization has serious problems. Forbus defined a quantity Q_1 to be greater than Q_2 over an interval, $\mathcal{I}$, if for all instants in the interval, $Q_1 > Q_2$ measured at that instant. Unfortunately, this definition has several problems. Since the quantification is over a single interval of time, it is impossible to make comparisons of systems whose time behavior changes as a result of a perturbation. Thus his attempt to formalize "distance equals rate times duration" in predicate calculus is severely limited. Rates can only be compared if the duration of an interval is unchanged.

But even if the quantification was correct, time-wise comparison is almost never a useful one to make. In the spring/block case, for example, it simply isn't the case that the heavy-block is always moving slower than the small-block; the periods get out of phase. The key to solving these problems is in the use of perspectives discussed earlier. The comparison on velocity (necessary to predict that the period lengthens) is valid only from the perspective of position.

5.5 Raiman's FOG

The formal basis for exaggeration was inspired by Raiman's FOG system for order of magnitude reasoning [48]. FOG is a representation that reduces qualitative reasoning ambiguity by explicitly modeling the fact

5.5. Raiman's FOG

that some parameters are negligible compared to others. Unlike previous attempts at order of magnitude reasoning, Raiman's rules are based on nonstandard analysis [49] and are, therefore, consistent. On the surface there appears to be considerable overlap between exaggeration and FOG, but in fact the systems are quite different. The main similarity is the shared foundation of nonstandard analysis and the hyperreal numbers, which results in a similar model of quantity space.

Although FOG does not represent a quantity space explicitly, it is implicit in the FOG relations: $\ll$ (infinitely less than), $\approx$ (infinitesimally close to), and $\sim$ (same order of magnitude)[1] These relations are as expressive as exaggeration's qualitative hyperreal representation with disjunction. For example, one can write $X \in (\text{HALO} \quad x_0 \ +)$ as $X \approx x_0 \ \wedge \ [X] = +$, and $X \in \prec 0, x_0 \succ$ is equivalent to

$$X \sim x_0 \ \wedge \ [X] = + \ \wedge \ Y = X + x_0 \ \wedge \ [Y] = - \ \wedge \ \neg Y \approx 0$$

The FOG expression $X \approx 0$ translates to:

$$X \in (\text{HALO} \quad 0 \ -) \ \vee \ X = 0 \ \vee \ X \in (\text{HALO} \quad 0 \ +)$$

Although the two representations are equivalent, one may be considerably more convenient than the other for a specific task. The brevity and specificity of the qualitative hyperreal representation is a big advantage for simulation.

But FOG is just an algebraic reasoner. Since it doesn't know about derivatives and integration, it cannot do qualitative simulation (as is required for exaggeration's simulate phase). Within the scope of algebraic reasoning, however, FOG's performance is impressive. Raiman poses the qualitative physics problem: "If two masses, one much smaller than the other, are moving towards each other with similar velocities, what will their velocities be after an elastic collision?" He demonstrates that approaches based on standard qualitative algebras are defeated by ambiguity. In contrast, FOG uses the assumption that one mass is negligible compared to the other to correctly predict that the velocity of the big mass will be relatively unaffected while the small mass will reverse direction and retreat at three times its original speed.

While this appears to be dynamical reasoning, it is not. The equations of motion for an elastic collision are discontinuous and thus cannot be

---

[1] Raiman's actual terms, Ne, Vo, and Co, are French abbreviations for the same relations [48].

differentiated. Instead, FOG solves the problem using explicit equations for conservation of energy and momentum. Extending FOG to perform qualitative simulation would be a major task, requiring (among other things) analogs of the predecessor-persistence filter and the successor-arrival filter.

5.6 Kuipers' Time Scale Abstraction

Time scale abstraction [39] is a technique for reducing ambiguity in qualitative simulation by modeling a complex system as a hierarchy of smaller, interacting equilibrium mechanisms. For example, Kuipers describes the kidney's sodium / water balance mechanisms in terms of two mechanisms that operate at different speeds. The water balance adjusts volume in a matter of minutes while the sodium balance adjusts sodium excretion over periods of hours and days. Kuipers observes that the amount of sodium appears constant to the water balance mechanism but the water mechanism seems to be instantaneous from the eyes of the sodium mechanism. Thus:

> When a faster mechanism views a slower one as being constant, the slower one can simply be treated as a source of values for certain parameters. When a slower mechanism views a faster one as instantaneous, a relation among shared variables may be treated by the fast mechanism as the result of a process over time, and by the slow mechanism as a functional relationship ([39, page 622]).

Kuipers extended QSIM [38] to handle mechanism hierarchies by switching between submodels, starting with the fastest time scale. An alternate way to simulate this hierarchical model would be to use HR-QSIM. By specifying sodium's derivative as negligible, the water mechanism would be guaranteed to reach equilibrium first, avoiding the intractable branching of a flat model. But I propose this solely to demonstrate the relationship between the two techniques. Kuipers' approach has the advantage that the time scale abstraction is explicit, not buried as it would be for HR-QSIM.

But there is an advantage to the HR-QSIM approach. Kuipers had to carefully hand construct his model hierarchy, manually assuring consistency of two views of the water balance mechanism: the fast model (a

QSIM structural description) and the slow model (a single constraint in the sodium mechanism). With the HR-QSIM approach, the abstraction assumption can be introduced automatically. For example, consider a flat model of the two mechanisms combined with no time scale information. If exaggeration were given the comparative analysis question "What if the sodium's 'velocity' were less?" then it would automatically generate a description of the system with the time scale abstraction. Unfortunately, exaggeration's simulate phase, HR-QSIM, could not take advantage of the abstraction since it is not explicit. The case is similar to that of the infinite flow rate heat exchanger discussed in section 4.5.2. Unifying the modeling abilities of exaggeration with the explicit representation of Kuipers' work is an important topic for future research.

5.7 Davis' CHEPACHET

Intrigued by my formulation of exaggeration (personal communication, [65]), Ernie Davis also approached the problem of order of magnitude solution of qualitative differential equations [4]. The resulting CHEPACHET program is a direct analog of exaggeration's simulate phase. HR-QSIM and CHEPACHET are very similar. In fact HR-QSIM's use of four transition tables (section 3.3.2) follows from Davis' temporal topology rule. The two programs appear to be equivalent in terms of systems they can simulate and ambiguities they filter. However, HR-QSIM uses a more expressive qualitative representation that is more appropriate for exaggeration.

Algorithm Differences CHEPACHET and HR-QSIM take different approaches to the qualitative simulation of qualitative differential equations: HR-QSIM does behavior generation while CHEPACHET produces an envisionment. HR-QSIM assumes a fixed initial state and produces the set of possible behaviors that could result from that initial specification. CHEPACHET, on the other hand, generates the graph of all possible states and the transitions between them, even if only a small subgraph is reachable from any initial state. Although the relative merits of the two approaches have been widely debated in the literature [22], it seems clear that both have advantages. Envisionments are more general, but also much larger and thus considerably more expensive to produce. Given the goal of exaggeration, behavior generation is the appropriate choice.

Although CHEPACHET and HR-QSIM take different approaches to temporal filtering, the approaches appear to be equivalent. In place of HR-QSIM's predecessor-persistence and successor-arrival filtering, CHEPACHET uses several inference rules based on the notion of a parameter's VARIANCE, how much the parameter is allowed to change during a time interval. The resulting inference rules are quite elegant—very simple (e.g., no need for HR-QSIM's infinite-distance arrival rule), yet powerful. Both HR-QSIM and CHEPACHET characterize a state in terms of four types of quantities. Both systems use the parameter's order of magnitude, the parameter's derivative order of magnitude, and the parameter's persistence time.[2] In addition, HR-QSIM uses the parameter's arrival time while CHEPACHET uses the parameter's variance. The one drawback to using variance measures rather than arrival times as this fourth quantity is its lack of physical significance. This complicates the process of understanding the reasons for CHEPACHET's predictions — an important liability since exaggeration is primarily an explanation technique.

Qualitative Representation CHEPACHET's qualitative representation is a subset of the qualitative hyperreal representation; landmarks other than zero are not allowed. In other words, there are seven possible values: ZERO, ±SMALL (infinitesimals), ±MEDIUM (finite, noninfinitesimal numbers, and ±LARGE (infinite numbers). Davis asserts [4] that it is easy to extend his representation to handle additional orders of magnitude (e.g., VERY-SMALL and VERY-LARGE), but this does not make up for the lack of multiple landmarks within a single order of magnitude.

To see the limitations of the CHEPACHET representation, consider the comparative analysis question "What happens to the output temperature of hot oil passing more quickly through a heat exchanger?" When HR-QSIM is given the description of oil moving infinitely fast, it predicts that the output heat will drop a negligible amount from q_0 to (HALO q_0 −). Since this is greater than the largest predicted value, $\prec 0, q_0 \succ$, in the case where oil velocity is finite, the scale phase can con-

---

[2] Davis calls it time duration or 'delta T' since he uses parametric variance instead of distinguishing between persistence and arrival times.

5.7. Davis' CHEPACHET

clude that output heat increases when flow rate increases.

But CHEPACHET could not support this deduction without some contortions. Assuming that CHEPACHET correctly predicts that Q does not transition to SMALL or ZERO when V is LARGE, there is still no way to compare the standard and hyperreal output values to see which is larger. Both $(\text{HALO} \quad q_0 \; -)$ and $\prec 0, q_0 \succ$ are represented as MEDIUM in the CHEPACHET representation.

One might argue that there is a simple fix to the problem: simply create a new parameter, Q-LOST, and add a constraint linking it to Q. This new parameter would distinguish the two cases by ending with a value of –SMALL when flow is infinite and –MEDIUM when oil velocity is finite. However, there are problems with adding extra parameters.

Who or what adds the new parameters to the model? This modeling step should not be lightly undertaken by a program, yet is an unattractive burden for a person. The addition of numerous new parameters complicates the model and makes it harder for people to understand and harder for programs to analyze. Extensions would be required to the scale phase if it were required to automatically analyze the Q-LOST parameter when asked a question about Q. Since an additional parameter is necessary for every landmark, this scheme would require the dynamic addition of parameters when new landmarks are added during simulation — an extra complication. In theory, the $\pm$LARGE, $\pm$MEDIUM, $\pm$SMALL, ZERO vocabulary is viable, but considerable work would be required to make it as easily expressive as the qualitative hyperreal representation. Because of this extra expressiveness, HR-QSIM is a more appropriate choice for exaggeration's simulate phase than CHEPACHET.

6 Conclusions

In this chapter, I summarize the main contribution of the book, suggest areas for future research, and present a few concluding remarks.

6.1 Summary

This book makes a number of contributions to the field of qualitative physics.

- It formalizes the problem of comparative analysis and distinguishes it from qualitative simulation.

- It solves the problems with previous treatments of relative change by explicitly accounting for multiple perspectives.

- It codifies the knowledge necessary for performing DQ analysis as a set of inference rules. The rules are proven sound and have been implemented using a forward chaining rule engine.

- It explains how the qualitative hyperreal representation extends Forbus' notion of quantity space [21] to handle infinitesimal and infinite hyperreal values.

- It presents predecessor-persistence and successor-arrival filtering and shows how they are used in a simulator that uses the qualitative hyperreal representation.

- It introduces exaggeration, a novel method for solving comparative analysis problems, and shows how qualitative hyperreal simulation is central to its operation.

- It compares the two comparative analytic techniques on a wide variety of dimensions so that future researchers can easily understand their strengths and weaknesses and use them effectively as black boxes.

6.2 Future Work

As is often the case, this work exposes new questions as it answers others. There are many areas that deserve further attention.

6.2.1 Augmenting DQ Analysis

As described in section 4.3.2, small changes in comparative analysis questions can render DQ analysis unable to answer. Three approaches show promise for increasing the coverage of DQ analysis:

- Since the DQ analysis rules match the system model syntax, small changes in the model (e.g., multiplication of a derivative by a constant) often result in decreases in competence. Can the models be converted into some kind of canonical form?

- Sometimes DQ analysis is able to deduce a relative change values for one parameter, but not for other parameters even if their value is determined by the first's. For example, DQ analysis determines that an increase in the fluid pump rate between two adjacent containers resulted in a greater equilibrium height difference (section 4.3.2) but is unable to conclude that this means one level is higher than before and the other lower. Integrating the algebraic methods of [74] would likely solve this and related problems.

- Proposition 21 states that relative change values over transition intervals are not exhaustive. Given a parameter X and a perspective P it is possible that neither $X\Uparrow_{(i,i+1)}^{P}$, nor $X\|_{(i,i+1)}^{P}$, nor $X\Downarrow_{(i,i+1)}^{P}$ is a true statement. As a result, DQ analysis cannot branch on the possible cases in the hopes of eliminating some through contradictions. However, relative change values at transitions (rather than the intervals between them) are exhaustive. It is not clear how great an advantage limited branching would be, but it would at least solve the pumped containers problem described in the bullet above.

6.2.2 Other Uses for Exaggeration

Although this book has treated exaggeration solely from the standpoint of a comparative analysis technique, exaggeration has a much greater potential.

Section 3.2.1 suggests how exaggeration might be used to solve a comparative analysis question that is not differential in nature: "Which heat exchanger can cool to a lower temperature, the regular or counterflow design?" The question is different from the other comparative analysis

6.2. Future Work

problems discussed because the difference between the two systems cannot be expressed as a differential change in a parameter. In one system velocity is positive and in the other it is negative. Exaggeration can be used to answer the question, but only through an obscure transformation. If the heat exchanger is infinitely long then the oil will be in thermal equilibrium as it exits. Thus in one oil will exit the counterflow exchanger at a lower temperature, the temperature at which the coolant enters. Future work should be spent on developing a theory of exaggeration's applicability to nondifferential comparative analysis problems. Specifically, what parameter should be transformed?

Another example of exaggeration's potential utility as a subroutine is shown by the comparative analysis problem: "When traveling a fixed distance in the rain, will you stay drier by running?" To model this situation, I make the following assumptions. The rain is falling straight down with uniform density. The person is a stick figure, leaning forward at an angle, θ, from vertical. Finally, the person only gets wet on his sides, not on the top of his head (which has zero area and is protected by a tiny hat anyway). Straight exaggeration might lead one to think that wetness is independent of speed. After all, if one were to move infinitely fast, one would get soaked by all the rain in the volume swept out. But if one moved with infinitesimal speed, then it would take an infinite time to get there and one's back would get soaked (remember that the figure is angled forward). This answer is incorrect because the system behaves nonmonotonically to changes in speed. In fact, exaggeration can be used to show that every angle, θ, specifies a unique speed that will allow the figure to traverse the distance without being touched by a single drop of rain. Suppose the person were prone, $\theta = 90°$, then if he could fly infinitely fast he wouldn't get touched. If the figure is completely vertical, $\theta = 0°$, then standing still keeps him dry; $\theta = negl$ degrees necessitates a negligible speed. Again, the question for research is how to choose the correct transformation and how to use the simulation results.

6.2.3 Reasoning about Discontinuous Systems

Although DQ analysis and exaggeration are both limited to continuous systems, many systems are discontinuous. How could the techniques of comparative analysis be extended to handle such systems? One possible approach would be to model the system in terms of piecewise continuous fragments. How would the individual models be created? How would an overall answer be composed from the trends of the pieces?

An interesting example (suggested by Paul Horwitz) to consider is that of a rocket navigating under the following, rather strange conditions. The rocket is not subject to gravity, but does experience linear friction: doubling initial velocity causes the rocket to go twice as far before coming to rest. If we assume that the space is one dimensional, the friction law can be written $V = V_0 - kX$. Finally, assume that instead of engines, the rocket has a keypad. When the pilot types an integer value, that number is added to the ships current velocity. The ship's initial velocity is zero.

If there is no friction, $k = 0$, then the rocket can stop at any position with the following simple procedure: type one on the keypad (or minus one if the desired point is to the left), wait until reaching the point, type minus one. However, if there is friction, then the rocket can only stop at certain discrete points. Clearly, one of these points is reached by typing one and waiting for friction to bring the ship to a halt at $X = x_0$. However, it may be less clear that there is no way to stop before x_0. Suppose the captain tries typing minus one halfway between the origin and x_0. Before typing the number, friction will have reduced the velocity from one to one half. Adding minus one to one half gives minus one half. Thus the ship will cruise back and stop at the origin. Any attempt to stop at a location other than Nx_0 for integer N is futile.

Now consider a comparative analysis question: "What happens to the distance between stopping points if friction is decreased?" Recalling the case for zero friction, one might be tempted to answer that the distance between resting points will decrease. In fact the opposite is true — halving the friction doubles the distance between stopping points. The mystery boils down to a simple discontinuity. If there is zero friction, one can stop anywhere, but if there is negligible friction, one can only stop at the origin and at infinity. Can a comparative analysis program make sense of system's like this?

6.2.4 Reasoning with Multiple Models

Despite the obvious utility of qualitative physics, there are serious problems with all qualitative reasoning techniques proposed so far. The inherent ambiguity of the qualitative algebra underlying these techniques seems to be unavoidable [60]. The resulting exponential branching limits qualitative simulation and comparative analysis techniques to small models of no more than a dozen parameters. Future work must focus on ways to reason about larger, more complex systems. One promising way to do this is by the use of multiple models of a system. Each model could encode a particular way of looking at the system (distinguished by different simplifying assumptions) appropriate for a specific class of problems. The following issues need to be solved. Given a problem, how is an appropriate model selected? Given a model and a solution generated from the model, how can one be sure that the solution is sufficient (in other words how can one be sure that the model was appropriate?) What structures the space of possible models? How can one switch between models?

Several researchers have done work that is relevant to this approach. Randy Davis' hardware troubleshooter [6] introduces more complex models of a circuit when simple models fail to explain the misbehavior. Patil's ABEL program [45] built multilevel causal descriptions of a human patient's illness. Kuipers models a kidney with time-scale abstraction [39] to reduce ambiguity. Weld's theory of aggregation [64] explains how new models of a system's behavior can be constructed dynamically and used in qualitative simulation. Collins and Forbus [3] discuss ways of integrating multiple models of fluid processes.

PROMPT [47] is a program which uses multiple models to perform innovative design [44]. This work introduced the notion of a graph of models (GoM). Each node in the graph denotes a model of the system at hand and the edge connecting two nodes is labeled with the set of simplifying assumptions (e.g., no friction) that distinguish the two models. Automated reasoning can be thought of as proceeding in three phases: 1) model selection, 2) quantitative analysis using the model, and 3) validation that the assumptions underlying the model were appropriate for the task at hand. If validation uncovers a discrepancy, this triggers domain-dependent parameter-change ruleparameter-change rules [1] which determine which assumptions should be retracted (i.e., where reasoning should proceed in the GoM).

SAM [67] can be thought of as a partial generalization of PROMPT. SAM also uses a GoM representation and also assumes that reasoning is divided into model slection, analysis, and validation phases. However, SAM uses RC values to represent discrepancies and uses inter-model comparative analysis instead of parameter-change rules when determining which assumptions to retract. Although inter-model comparative analysis is very difficult in general, it is shown that if the GoM edges are restricted to a particular class of assumptions (called APPROXIMATION REFORMULATIONS) then inter-model comparative analysis reduces to the standard forms discussed in this book. As a result, the techniques of DQ analysis and exaggeration can be used to direct model-switching.

Falkenhainer and Forbus have developed an alternate paradigm for multiple perspective, multi-granular modeling [20]. Instead of a graph of models, Falkenhainer and Forbus define a generating set of model pieces that can be turned on and off by CONSIDER ASSUMPTIONS. By alternately assuming all consistent sets of consider assumptions, one could produce a graph of models, but by not doing so explicitly, considerable space savings are realized. In addition, Falkenhainer and Forbus introduce the important distinction between simplifying and operating assumptions. Simplifying assumptions abstract details from the device model while operating assumptions limit consideration to subcases of behavior such as equilibrium operation. They demonstrate the power of their approach by describing an implemented question-answering program that considers only pertinent aspects of a Navy steam propulsion plant model for each question.

6.2.5 Mixed Qualitative Quantitative Reasoning

While qualitative reasoning has its place, it isn't appropriate for quantitative problems. For some time researchers have given lip service to the problem of integrating the two approaches, but little has been done. Simmons' quantity lattice [58] and Sacks' QMR program [51] are notable exceptions. The key issue is not so much developing a representation which unifies both types of reasoning, rather understanding when each is appropriate, and knowing how one type of reasoning affects the model for the other. Thus this area of work has much in common with that of the previous section.

6.3 Conclusions

DQ analysis and exaggeration have been tested on dozens of simple comparative analysis examples from the domains of mechanics, thermodynamics and electronics. Both techniques can be used to generate symbolic explanations for how and why the behavior of a system will

6.3. Conclusions

change given a structural perturbation. Both techniques work well on many, but not all comparative analysis questions.

DQ analysis is sound; whenever it deduces an answer, the answer is guaranteed to be correct. Exaggeration, on the other hand, will frequently answer incorrectly for systems in which the perturbation causes nonmonotonic changes in parameter values. Unfortunately, there appears to be no general, qualitative method of ensuring that a system reacts monotonically.

On the other hand, exaggeration appears to solve many more comparative analysis problems than does DQ analysis. Both techniques solve some problems that stump the other, but exaggeration has the upper hand. The difference lies in DQ analysis' reliance on syntactic matching of rules to the differential equation model. To handle every case, DQ analysis would need to solve the intractable problem of simplifying equations to canonical form. Exaggeration, however, needs only to evaluate the equations, not prove them equivalent, to predict relative change values.

The two techniques complementary strengths suggest a powerful high level architecture. Given a problem, first try to solve it with DQ analysis. If that works, then a sound answer is guaranteed. If DQ analysis fails, then apply exaggeration. Now check exaggeration's predictions with all of the relative change values that DQ analysis is able to deduce. If they all agree, the chances are good that nonmonotonic behavior is absent. Finally, exaggerate the perturbation in the opposite direction and check that the resulting predictions are the opposite of the first transformation. Although there will still be pathological cases, these precautions maximize the heuristic power of the exaggeration method.

A Glossary

The glossary starts with a list of symbol types that clarifies some of the math in this thesis, then moves on to specific terms in alphabetic order. Whenever appropriate a reference is made to the best description of the term in the text.

Caligraphic Letters Denote sets of real or hyperreal numbers, except $\mathcal{S}$ which denotes a qualitative state and $\mathcal{T}$ which denote a function from transitions to times. (Section 2.1.2).

Lowercase Letters Denote specific real or hyperreal values. For example, v_0 might be the initial velocity of some object.

Uppercase Greek Letters Denote qualitative values.

Uppercase Letters Denote parameters in a system. For example, V frequently denotes velocity. (Section 2.1).

$\prec a, b \succ$ Signifies an open interval of finite numbers between a and b and not including the infinitesimals surrounding a or b. (Section 3.1.2).

$\hat{}$ Signifies the perturbed system.

γ_i The ith transition. See transition.

$\Uparrow$ The relative change value signifying that the perturbed system is greater than the original. (Section 2.1.2).

$\|$ The relative change value signifying that the perturbed system is equal to the original. (Section 2.1.2).

$\Downarrow$ The relative change value signifying that the perturbed system is less than the original. (Section 2.1.2).

ARK A version of AMORD used to implement DQ analysis.

Behavior A sequence of qualitative states. (Section 2.1).

Behavioral Topology The ordered sequence of transitions that distinguishes one behavior from other possible paths through the tree of states produced by the qualitative simulator. (Section 2.5).

CO-transition A change in value from a closed point to an open interval. (Section 3.3.2).

Covering Perspective A parameter which is strictly monotonic over an interval between two transitions and which has the same value at both transitions in both the original and perturbed systems. (Section 2.1.3).

dec Signifies that a parameter is decreasing, i.e. its derivative is negative.

DISTANCE The distance between two qualitative hyperreal values. For example, the distance between (HALO 0 +) and ≺0, *inf*≻ is *fin*. Used by the successor-arrival filter. (Section 3.3.5).

Distance-Rate-Time Table A table for computing the time required to traverse a given distance (or width) at a given rate. (Figure 3.11 in section 3.3.4).

Distinguished Time Point The time when a parameter reaches a landmark value. (Section 2.1).

Duration Rule The duration rule formalizes "distance equals rate times time" for DQ analysis. (Section 2.2.1).

fin Finite. An order of magnitude: greater than all infinitesimals but smaller than any infinite number.

HALO Every real number has a halo of hyperreal numbers surrounding it, infinitesimally closely. (Section 3.1.2).

HR-QDIR Hyperreal qualitative direction: a pair of a standard qualitative direction (*inc*, *dec*, or *std*) and an order of magnitude. (Section 3.1.2).

HR-QR The hyperreal qualitative representation of a parameter's state consisting of the pair of the parameter's value and its derivative: (HR-QVAL, HR-QDIR). (Section 3.1.2).

HR-QSIM An implementation of the simulate phase of exaggeration. The hyperreal qualitative simulator. (Section 3.3).

HR-QVAL A hyperreal qualitative value, for example a landmark value, a halo, a finite interval, *inf*, or *minf*. (Section 3.1.2).

Hyperreal Numbers The field of numbers which include the standard reals as well as infinitesimals and infinities. (Section 3.1.1).

inc Signifies that a parameter is increasing, i.e. its derivative is positive.

inf Infinity. Both an order of magnitude and a possible value in the qualitative hyperreal representation. (Section 3.1.1).

Infinite Arrival Rule A rule which says that a parameter will take only negligible time to reach infinity from a finite value if it is going infinitely fast. (Section 17).

Interval Derivative Rule A rule that expresses the relationship between one derivative and another, e.g., "greater acceleration leads to higher velocity." (Section 2.2.2).

Landmark Value An important qualitative value of a parameter. Often distinguished by the modeler, but sometimes deduced by a program. (Section 2.1).

minf Minus infinity a possible value in the qualitative hyperreal representation. (Section 3.1.1).

negl Negligible. Both an order of magnitude and a possible value in the qualitative hyperreal representation. The same thing as infinitesimal. (Section 3.1.1).

Next Value Tables Tables used to generate the possible next values of each parameter. (Section 3.3.2).

Nonstandard Analysis A theory of calculus developed by Abraham Robinson that gives a consistent formalization of the notion of infinitesimal numbers. (Appendix C).

NS-transition A change in value from a nonstandard open interval to a standard open interval. For example, from inf to $\prec 0, inf \succ$ (Section 3.3.2).

OC-transition A change in value from an open interval to a closed point. (Section 3.3.2).

OM The order of magnitude part of the qualitative hyperreal representation of derivative. (Section 3.1.2).

Parameter Defined as a reasonable function of time. Used to represent a variable in a system. For example, V frequently denotes velocity as a function of time. (Section 2.1).

Partial Perspective A parameter which is strictly monotonic over an interval between two transitions, but which does not necessarily have the same value at both transitions in both the original and perturbed systems. (Section 2.1.3).

Perspective See partial perspective.

Predecessor-Persistence Filter A simulation technique for eliminating inconsistent states by checking the amount of time a parameter's qualitative value persists. (Section 3.3.4).

QDIR QSIM's qualitative representation for the direction a parameter is moving. Either *inc, dec,* or *std*. (Section 2.1).

QS A QSIM qualitative state. (Section 2.1).

QSIM Kuipers' program for qualitative simulation [38].

Qualitative Hyperreal Representation An extended quantity space representation that includes infinitesimal and infinite values. Used by exaggeration. (Section 3.1.2).

QVAL QSIM Qualitative value. (Section 2.1).

Relative Change A notation used by DQ analysis to describe how a parameter changes value. Possible values are: $\Uparrow$, $\Downarrow$, and $\|$. (Section 2.1.2).

RC See relative change.

$\mathcal{S}$ A variable denoting a qualitative state.

Scale Phase The final phase of exaggeration which compares standard and hyperreal qualitative behaviors to answer a comparative analysis question. (Section 3.4).

Simulate Phase The middle phase of exaggeration which simulates the exaggerated system produced by the transform phase. (Section 3.3).

SN-transition A change in value from a standard open interval to a nonstandard open interval. For example, from $\prec 0, \mathit{inf}\succ$ to inf. (Section 3.3.2).

State Tree The tree of states generated by QSIM or HR-QSIM. Any path through this tree is a behavior.

std Signifies that a parameter is not changing, i.e. its derivative is zero.

Structural Description A set of qualitative differential equations that relates the various parameters in a system. (Section 2.1).

Successor-Arrival Filter A simulation technique for eliminating inconsistent states by checking the amount of time a parameter takes to arrive at the next qualitative value. (Section 3.3.5).

System A group of parameters related by a structural description. (Section 2.1).

$\mathcal{T}$ The time function, which takes transitions to the times when they occur. (Section 2.1.2).

Topologically Equal See behavioral topology.

Transform Phase The first phase of exaggeration. It takes the perturbation from the comparative analysis problem and constructs and exaggerated system description which is simulated by the simulate phase. (Section 3.2).

Transition The event when a parameter changes from one qualitative value to another. A transitions is written as a lowercase gamma: γ. (Section 2.1).

WIDTH The qualitative value of the maximum difference between two hyperreal numbers that share a qualitative hyperreal value. For example, the width of (HALO 0 +) is *negl*. (Section 3.3.4).

B A Useful Example

This section constructs an example which serves both as a counter-example for a generalized version of the derivative rule and as the proof of the non-exhaustive proposition. Suppose that A, V, and X are parameters such that $A = \frac{d}{dt}V$, $V = \frac{d}{dt}X$, and X is a covering perspective over (γ_i, γ_{i+1}). The derivative rule (proposition 3) showed that if A and V are positive over the interval (γ_i, γ_{i+1}) and if $\neg V \Uparrow_i$, and $A \Downarrow_{(i,i+1)}^X$, then $V \Downarrow_{(i,i+1)}^X$.

Unfortunately, the derivative rule is not true for arbitrary perspectives. The following abberation should convince you of this. I show three parameters, V, A, and P such that $A = \frac{d}{dt}V$ and P is a covering perspective over (γ_0, γ_1). Yet although $A\|_{(0,1)}^P$ the parameter V has no consistent behavior from the perspective of P. During part of the interval $V \Uparrow^P$ and during part $V \Downarrow^P$.

Here are the details. Over the absolute time interval $(0, 1)$ define:

$V(t) = \frac{1}{2}t^2$
$A(t) = \frac{d}{dt}V(t) = t \qquad A^{-1}(a) = a$
$P(t) = A(t) = t \qquad P^{-1}(p) = p$
$\widehat{V}(t) = \frac{1}{3}t^3$
$\widehat{A}(t) = \frac{d}{dt}\widehat{V}(t) = t^2 \qquad \widehat{A}^{-1}(a) = a^{\frac{1}{2}}$
$\widehat{P}(t) = \widehat{A}(t) = t^2 \qquad \widehat{P}^{-1}(p) = p^{\frac{1}{2}}$

Note that $P(0) = \widehat{P}(0) = 0$ and $P(1) = \widehat{P}(1) = 1$ and P is strictly monotonic, so P is a valid perspective over this interval. Since $P = A$ and $\widehat{P} = \widehat{A}$ the self reference theorem shows that $A\|_{(0,1)}^P$. So what does V do from the perspective of P? Consider $p = \frac{1}{9}$:

$$V(P^{-1}(p)) = \frac{1}{2}p^2 = \frac{1}{162}, \quad \text{and} \quad \widehat{V}(\widehat{P}^{-1}(p)) = \frac{1}{3}p^{\frac{3}{2}} = \frac{1}{81}$$

Now let $p = \frac{8}{9}$:

$$V(P^{-1}(p)) = \frac{1}{2}p^2 = \frac{32}{81}, \quad \text{and} \quad \widehat{V}(\widehat{P}^{-1}(p)) = \frac{1}{3}p^{\frac{3}{2}} = \frac{16\sqrt{2}}{81} < \frac{32}{81}$$

So for a small value of p the corresponding $\widehat{v}$ is larger than v, but for larger p the situation is reversed. Thus it is neither the case that $V\Uparrow_{(0,1)}^P$ nor $V\|_{(0,1)}^P$ nor $V\Downarrow_{(0,1)}^P$ even though $A\|_{(0,1)}^P$.

C Readings in Nonstandard Analysis

There are a wide variety of sources for people who wish to learn more about nonstandard analysis, but most of them are old or out of print. A Scientific American article [5] by Davis and Hersh is a good starting point; it provides a good history and flavor for the material but does not present any technical details. Henle and Kleinberg [32] have a book designed for use in a freshman calculus class. Assuming no mathematical background, it defines the infinitesimals and shows how they can be used to define derivatives and integrals. The book is easy to understand, but is so slow and devoid of proofs that it is rather frustrating to read. Keisler has two books on the subject. One is similar to Henle and Kleinberg, an alternative book for college freshman, the other, [35], is for teachers who are using the first. This teacher's guide is the best book for people who are mathematically literate yet not experts. Specifically, no background in model theory is required. The treatment is elegant and all theorems are proven. Robinson [49] is the classic source as he figured it all out. Unfortunately, his text assumes considerable sophistication and a strong background in model theory.

D HR-QSIM Transition Tables

This section contains the procedural encoding of the qualitative hyperreal transition tables discussed in section 3.3.2. There are four types of transitions: CO-transitions have a topology which is closed on the left yet open on the right, OC-transitions are open on the left and closed on the right, and both NS- and SN-transitions have an open-open topology.

Each of the transition functions takes four arguments: hr-qval is the parameter's current value (e.g., (HALO 0 +)), qdir and om are the two components of the parameter's current HR-QDIR (e.g., *inc* and *negl*), and qspace is the parameter's quantity space, i.e., an ordered list of its landmark values. Each of the transition functions returns a list of possible next values. The car of each 'next-value' is the HR-QVAL and the cadr is the HR-QDIR, represented as a two element list: (qdir om). Since finite intervals are represented as two element lists, they look indistinguishable from QSIM open intervals.[1] Thus the qualitative hyperreal representation $(\prec 0, inf \succ, (dec\ negl))$ is represented by the following list: ((0 inf) (dec neg)).

```
(defun CO-TRANSITIONS (hr-qval qdir om qspace)
  (ignore qspace)
  (if (landmark? hr-qval)                     ; QVAL closed - can chng
      (if (eql qdir 'std)                     ; QDIR can change too
          (list '((halo ,hr-qval +) (inc neg))
                '((halo ,hr-qval -) (dec neg))
                '(,hr-qval           (std 0)))
          (list '((halo ,hr-qval ,(if (eql qdir 'inc) '+ '-))
                  (,qdir ,om))))
      ;; else HR-QVAL is not closed and can't change.
      (if (eql qdir 'std)
          (list '(,hr-qval (std 0))           ; HR-QDIR can change
                '(,hr-qval (inc neg))
                '(,hr-qval (dec neg)))
          (list '(,hr-qval (,qdir ,om))))))   ; HR-QDIR can't change
```

---

[1] The representation is unique, however, because open intervals are not used by HR-QSIM.

Appendix D. HR-QSIM Transition Tables

```
(defun OC-TRANSITIONS (hr-qval qdir om qspace)
  (ignore qspace)
  (if (and (landmark? hr-qval)
           (member qdir '(inc dec)))
      nil                                        ; Must change but can't
      (product-space
        (list (cons hr-qval                      ; Old QVAL still ok
                    (if (and (halo? hr-qval)
                             (or (and (eql qdir 'inc)
                                      (eql (caddr hr-qval) '-))
                                 (and (eql qdir 'dec)
                                      (eql (caddr hr-qval) '+))))
                        (list (cadr hr-qval))    ; Halo center also pos
                        nil))                    ; No other possble QVALs
              (cons '(,qdir ,om)                 ; Old QDIR is always ok
                    (if (eql om 'neg)
                        '((std 0))               ; Also param could stop
                        nil))))))                ; Not in this case




(defun NS-TRANSITIONS (hr-qval qdir om qspace)
  (cond ((eql qdir 'std)
         (list '((,hr-qval (,qdir ,om))))        ; No change pos
        ((landmark? hr-qval)
         nil)                                    ; Inconsistent
        ((or (finite-interval? hr-qval)          ; Stan QVAL can't
             (and (eql hr-qval 'inf)  (eql qdir 'inc)) ; Nor these nonstan
             (and (eql hr-qval 'minf) (eql qdir 'dec))
             (and (halo? hr-qval) (or (and (eql (caddr hr-qval) '+)
                                           (eql qdir 'dec))
                                      (and (eql (caddr hr-qval) '-)
                                           (eql qdir 'inc)))))
         (product-space (list '(,hr-qval)
                              (ns-hr-qdir-transitions qdir om))))
        (t                                       ; Nons that can chng
         (let ((alt (cond ((eql hr-qval 'minf)
                           '(minf ,(succ 'minf qspace)))
                          ((eql hr-qval 'inf)
                           '(,(pred 'inf qspace) inf))
                          ((eql (caddr hr-qval) '+)
                           '(,(cadr hr-qval)
                             ,(succ (cadr hr-qval) qspace)))
                          ((eql (caddr hr-qval) '-)
                           '(,(pred (cadr hr-qval) qspace)
                             ,(cadr hr-qval))))))
           (product-space (list '(,hr-qval ,alt)
                                (ns-hr-qdir-transitions qdir om)))))))
```

```
(defun SN-TRANSITIONS (hr-qval qdir om qspace)
  (ignore qspace)
  (cond ((eql qdir 'std)                      ; Deriv can't change
         (list '(,hr-qval (,qdir ,om))))      ; ... so HR-QVAL stuck
        ((landmark? hr-qval)
         nil)                                 ; Must change but can't
        ((finite-interval? hr-qval)           ; These can change
         (let ((alt (cond ((and (eql qdir 'inc)
                                (eql (cadr hr-qval) 'inf))
                           'inf)
                          ((and (eql qdir 'dec)
                                (eql (car  hr-qval) 'minf))
                           'minf)
                          ((eql qdir 'inc) '(halo ,(cadr hr-qval) -))
                          (t               '(halo ,(car hr-qval) +)))))
           (product-space (list '(,hr-qval ,alt)
                                (sn-hr-qdir-transitions qdir om)))))
        (t                                    ; Nonstan QVALs can't chng
         (product-space (list '(,hr-qval)
                              (sn-hr-qdir-transitions qdir om))))))
```

The following two utility functions determine whether a parameter's HR-QDIR can change given the type of transition (NS- or SN-) being considered. For example, if a HR-QDIR changes from (*inc negl*) to (*inc fin*) that is an NS- transition since the parameter's derivative must have transitioned from (HALO 0 +) to ≺0, *inf*≻ for the HR-QDIR to change. Since the system model may not have provided an explicit parameter name for the derivative, it is best to check derivative transitions at this point rather than count on constraint filtering to eliminate inconsistencies.

```
(defun NS-HR-QDIR-TRANSITIONS (qdir om)
  (case om
    (0   '((,qdir ,om)))
    (neg '((,qdir ,om) (,qdir fin)))
    (fin '((,qdir ,om)))                      ; HR-QDIR can't change
    (inf '((,qdir ,om) (,qdir fin)))))

(defun SN-HR-QDIR-TRANSITIONS (qdir om)
  (case om
    (0   '((,qdir ,om)))
    (neg '((,qdir ,om)))
    (fin '((,qdir ,om) (,qdir neg) (,qdir inf)))
    (inf '((,qdir ,om)))))
```

E Program Output for the Spring and Block

This chapter shows the actual behavior of the current implementation of DQ analysis and exaggeration on the example of a block attached to a spring on a horizontal, frictionless table. The model includes explicit energy conservation equations to reduce ambiguity. The next section presents the actual code input description. Following sections show the output generated by the two techniques given an increase in the mass of the block.

E.1 Model of the System

```
(define-QDE LINEAR-SPRING-W-EC           ; Qual. Differential Eq.
   (print-names (A  "Acceleration")
                (V  "Velocity")
                (X  "Position")
                (F  "Force")
                (M  "Mass")
                (K  "Spring Constant"))
                (VV "Velocity Squared"))
                (KE "Kinetic Energy"))
                (PE "Potential Energy"))
                (TE "Total Energy"))
   (independent M K TE)                  ; These params are constants
   (dependent A X V F VV KE PE)          ; These params may change
   (boundary X V M K)                    ; These may be perturbed
   (constraints ((d//dt X V))            ; Vel = time deriv of pos
                ((d//dt V A))            ; Definition of acceleration
                ((mult M A F))           ; Newton's 2nd law of motion
                ((mult X K F))           ; Hooke's law
                ((mult V V VV))          ; Defn of velocity squared
                ((mult VV M KE))         ; Defn of kinetic energy
                ((mult F F PE))          ; Cheating definition of PE
                ((add PE KE TE)))        ; Definition of total energy
   (quantity-spaces (K  (minf k* 0 inf)) ; Spring const k* = negative
                    (M  (minf 0 m* inf))  ;
                    (TE (minf 0 te* inf)))) ; Landmark te* is positive

(define-init RELEASE-DISPLACED           ; Named initial conditions
              linear-spring-w-ec         ; for this qual. diff. eq.
   ((X ((minf 0) std))                   ; X initially tween minf, 0
    (F ((0 inf) std))
    (A ((0 inf) std))
    (TE (te* std))
    (M (m* std))                         ; Mass steady at landmark m*
    (K (k* std))
    (V (0 inc))))                        ; V is zero but increasing
```

E.2 DQ Analysis Output

When the user selects the model shown above, the CA program applies QSIM to it, producing a single behavior corresponding to stable oscillation. Next a propositional encoding of the model, the behavior, and a perturbation ($M\Uparrow_0$) are loaded into the database. Then ARK applies inference rules to deduce as many relative change values as possible. When no more rules match, the database contents are displayed. For simplicity, only relevant database propositions are printed (e.g., the propositional encoding of the system behavior is not).

```
Time: 0
      (RC V 0 DEQ)
      (RC X 0 DEQ)
      (RC M 0 DUP)            ; This is the initial perturbation
      (RC K 0 DEQ)            ; Spring constant unchanged
      (RC F 0 DEQ)
      (RC A 0 DDN)            ; Acceleration initially down
      (RC PE 0 DEQ)
      (RC VV 0 DEQ)
      (RC KE 0 DEQ)
      (RC TE 0 DEQ)
Time: (0 1)
      (RC V (0 1) DDN (C- X))     ; V down from the perspective X
      (RC V (0 1) DDN (C- F))     ; 'C-' means covering perspective
      (RC V (0 1) DDN (C- PE))
      (RC V (0 1) DDN (C- KE))
      (RC X (0 1) DEQ (C- X))
      (RC X (0 1) DEQ (C- F))
      (RC X (0 1) DEQ (C- PE))
      (RC X (0 1) DEQ (C- KE))
      (RC M (0 1) DUP (C- X))
      (RC M (0 1) DUP (C- F))
      (RC M (0 1) DUP (C- PE))
      (RC M (0 1) DUP (C- KE))
      (RC K (0 1) DEQ (C- X))
      (RC K (0 1) DEQ (C- F))
      (RC K (0 1) DEQ (C- PE))
      (RC K (0 1) DEQ (C- KE))
      (RC F (0 1) DEQ (C- X))
      (RC F (0 1) DEQ (C- F))
      (RC F (0 1) DEQ (C- PE))
      (RC F (0 1) DEQ (C- KE))
      (RC A (0 1) DDN (C- X))     ; A down from the perspective X
      (RC A (0 1) DDN (C- F))
      (RC A (0 1) DDN (C- PE))
      (RC A (0 1) DDN (C- KE))
      (RC PE (0 1) DEQ (C- X))
      (RC PE (0 1) DEQ (C- F))
```

E.2. DQ Analysis Output

```
        (RC PE (0 1) DEQ (C- PE))
        (RC PE (0 1) DEQ (C- KE))
        (RC VV (0 1) DDN (C- X))
        (RC VV (0 1) DDN (C- F))
        (RC VV (0 1) DDN (C- PE))
        (RC VV (0 1) DDN (C- KE))
        (RC KE (0 1) DEQ (C- X))
        (RC KE (0 1) DEQ (C- F))
        (RC KE (0 1) DEQ (C- PE))
        (RC KE (0 1) DEQ (C- KE))
        (RC TE (0 1) DEQ (C- X))
        (RC TE (0 1) DEQ (C- F))
        (RC TE (0 1) DEQ (C- PE))
        (RC TE (0 1) DEQ (C- KE))
        (DURATION (0 1) DUP)           ; Thus it takes longer!
        (DISTANCE-BY K (0 1) DEQ)
        (DISTANCE-BY PE (0 1) DEQ)
        (DISTANCE-BY F (0 1) DEQ)
        (DISTANCE-BY A (0 1) DDN)
        (DISTANCE-BY X (0 1) DEQ)      ; X moves same distance
        (DISTANCE-BY TE (0 1) DEQ)
        (DISTANCE-BY KE (0 1) DEQ)
        (DISTANCE-BY V (0 1) DDN)
        (DISTANCE-BY VV (0 1) DDN)
Time: 1
        (RC V 1 DDN)                   ; Maximum velocity is lower
        (RC X 1 DEQ)
        (RC M 1 DUP)
        (RC K 1 DEQ)
        (RC F 1 DEQ)
        (RC A 1 DEQ)
        (RC PE 1 DEQ)
        (RC T 1 DUP)                   ; Time of transition is bigger
        (RC VV 1 DDN)                  ; Although V squared is less...
        (RC KE 1 DEQ)                  ; Kinetic energy is the same
        (RC TE 1 DEQ)
```

One can ask to see the justification for any proposition in the database. Below I list the dependency tree for the assertion that it takes longer for the heavier block to reach rest position. Unlike the display above, here I show all propositions in the tree regardless of their importance. The subexpression '(P- X)' means that the parameter X is a partial perspective.

```
(DURATION (0 1) DUP) is IN due to DURATION-THEOREM1:
  (OPPOSITE-RC DDN DUP) is IN because it's a PREMISE
  (DISTANCE-BY X (0 1) DEQ) is IN due to DISTANCE:
    (SIGN X (0 1) -) is IN because it's a PREMISE
    (RC X 0 DEQ) is IN because it's a PREMISE
    (RC X 1 DEQ) is IN due to ZERO-DOES-NOT-CHANGE:
```

```
        (QMAG X 1 0) is IN because it's a PREMISE
        (TRANSITION-POINT 1) is IN because it's a PREMISE
  (RC V (0 1) DDN (P- X)) is IN due to DERIVATIVE-THEOREM1:
    (OTHER-RC DDN + DDN) is IN because it's a PREMISE
    (OTHER-RC DDN + DDN) is IN  ===already explained===
    (SIGN V (0 1) +) is IN because it's a PREMISE
    (SIGN A (0 1) +) is IN because it's a PREMISE
    (RC A (0 1) DDN (P- X)) is IN due to MULT-INT-B:
      (MULT M A F) is IN because it's a PREMISE
      (RC M (0 1) DUP (P- X)) is IN due to WEAKEN-PERSP-RC-VALUES:
        (RC M (0 1) DUP (C- X)) is IN due to INTERVAL-CONSTANT-THEOREM:
          (RC M 0 DUP) is IN because it's a PREMISE
          (QDIR M (0 1) STD) is IN because it's a PREMISE
          (PERSPECTIVE (C- X) (0 1)) is IN due to COVERING-PERSP-DEFN:
            (RC X 0 DEQ) is IN  ===already explained===
            (RC X 1 DEQ) is IN  ===already explained===
            (PERSPECTIVE (P- X) (0 1)) is IN due to PARTIAL-PERSP-DEFN1:
              (QDIR X (0 1) INC) is IN because it's a PREMISE
      (RC F (0 1) DEQ (P- X)) is IN due to MULT-INT-C:
        (MULT X K F) is IN because it's a PREMISE
        (RC X (0 1) DEQ (P- X)) is IN due to WEAKEN-PERSP-RC-VALUES:
          (RC X (0 1) DEQ (C- X)) is IN due to SELF-REFERENCE:
            (PERSPECTIVE (C- X) (0 1)) is IN  ===already explained===
        (RC K (0 1) DEQ (P- X)) is IN due to WEAKEN-PERSP-RC-VALUES:
          (RC K (0 1) DEQ (C- X)) is IN due to INTERVAL-CONSTANT-THEOREM:
            (RC K 0 DEQ) is IN because it's a PREMISE
            (QDIR K (0 1) STD) is IN because it's a PREMISE
            (PERSPECTIVE (C- X) (0 1)) is IN  ===already explained===
      (SIGN X (0 1) -) is IN  ===already explained===
      (SIGN K (0 1) -) is IN because it's a PREMISE
    (RC A 0 DDN) is IN due to MULT-POINT-B:
      (MULT M A F) is IN  ===already explained===
      (RC M 0 DUP) is IN  ===already explained===
      (RC F 0 DEQ) is IN due to MULT-POINT-C:
        (MULT X K F) is IN  ===already explained===
        (RC X 0 DEQ) is IN  ===already explained===
        (RC K 0 DEQ) is IN  ===already explained===
    (RC V 0 DEQ) is IN because it's a PREMISE
    (RC X 0 DEQ) is IN  ===already explained===
    (D//DT V A) is IN because it's a PREMISE
    (D//DT X V) is IN because it's a PREMISE
  (D//DT X V) is IN  ===already explained===
```

E.3   Exaggeration Output

Given the perturbation $M \Uparrow_0$ the transform phase of exaggeration creates a new state, XS60, to encode the exaggerated initial conditions (i.e. infinite mass). HR-QSIM generates four possible behaviors one of which is shown below.

```
State XS60 persisting(0), and arriving (NEG):
```

E.3. Exaggeration Output

```
        PE   : PE1          (STD 0)
        KE   : 0            (STD 0)
        VV   : 0            (STD 0)
        F    : F2           (STD 0)
        A    : (HALO 0 +)   (STD 0)
        V    : 0            (INC NEG)
        X    : X15          (STD 0)
State XS61 persisting(INF FIN NEG), and arriving (INF):
        PE   : (HALO PE1 -)  (DEC NEG)
        KE   : (HALO 0 +)    (INC NEG)
        VV   : (HALO 0 +)    (INC NEG)
        F    : (HALO F2 -)   (DEC NEG)
        A    : (HALO 0 +)    (DEC NEG)
        V    : (HALO 0 +)    (INC NEG)
        X    : (HALO X15 +)  (INC NEG)
State XS63 persisting(INF), and arriving (INF):
        PE   : (0 PE1)       (DEC NEG)
        KE   : (0 INF)       (INC NEG)
        VV   : (HALO 0 +)    (INC NEG)
        F    : (0 F2)        (DEC NEG)
        A    : (HALO 0 +)    (DEC NEG)
        V    : (HALO 0 +)    (INC NEG)
        X    : (X15 0)       (INC NEG)
State XS65 persisting(INF FIN NEG), and arriving (INF FIN NEG):
        PE   : (HALO 0 +)    (DEC NEG)
        KE   : (0 INF)       (INC NEG)
        VV   : (HALO 0 +)    (INC NEG)
        F    : (HALO 0 +)    (DEC NEG)
        A    : (HALO 0 +)    (DEC NEG)
        V    : (HALO 0 +)    (INC NEG)
        X    : (HALO 0 -)    (INC NEG)
State XS67 persisting(0), and arriving (NEG):
        PE   : 0             (STD 0)
        KE   : KE1           (STD 0)
        VV   : (HALO 0 +)    (STD 0)
        F    : 0             (DEC NEG)
        A    : 0             (DEC NEG)
        V    : (HALO 0 +)    (STD 0)
        X    : 0             (INC NEG)
State XS69 persisting(INF FIN), and arriving (INF):
        PE   : (HALO 0 +)    (INC NEG)
        KE   : (HALO KE1 -)  (DEC NEG)
        VV   : (HALO 0 +)    (DEC NEG)
        F    : (HALO 0 -)    (DEC NEG)
        A    : (HALO 0 -)    (DEC NEG)
        V    : (HALO 0 +)    (DEC NEG)
        X    : (HALO 0 +)    (INC NEG)
State XS71 persisting(INF), and arriving (INF):
```

```
           PE   : (0 PE1)       (INC NEG)
           KE   : (0 KE1)       (DEC NEG)
           VV   : (HALO 0 +)    (DEC NEG)
           F    : (MINF 0)      (DEC NEG)
           A    : (HALO 0 -)    (DEC NEG)
           V    : (HALO 0 +)    (DEC NEG)
           X    : (0 INF)       (INC NEG)

State XS73 persisting(INF FIN NEG), and arriving (INF FIN NEG):
           PE   : (HALO PE1 -)  (INC NEG)
           KE   : (HALO 0 +)    (DEC NEG)
           VV   : (HALO 0 +)    (DEC NEG)
           F    : (MINF 0)      (DEC NEG)
           A    : (HALO 0 -)    (DEC NEG)
           V    : (HALO 0 +)    (DEC NEG)
           X    : (0 INF)       (INC NEG)

State XS75 persisting(0), and arriving (NEG):
           PE   : PE1           (STD 0)
           KE   : 0             (STD 0)
           VV   : 0             (STD 0)
           F    : F3            (STD 0)
           A    : (HALO 0 -)    (STD 0)
           V    : 0             (DEC NEG)
           X    : X16           (STD 0)

State XS77 persisting(INF FIN), and arriving (INF):
           PE   : (HALO PE1 -)  (DEC NEG)
           KE   : (HALO 0 +)    (INC NEG)
           VV   : (HALO 0 +)    (INC NEG)
           F    : (HALO F3 +)   (INC NEG)
           A    : (HALO 0 -)    (INC NEG)
           V    : (HALO 0 -)    (DEC NEG)
           X    : (HALO X16 -)  (DEC NEG)

State XS80 persisting(INF), and arriving (INF):
           PE   : (0 PE1)       (DEC NEG)
           KE   : (0 KE1)       (INC NEG)
           VV   : (HALO 0 +)    (INC NEG)
           F    : (F3 0)        (INC NEG)
           A    : (HALO 0 -)    (INC NEG)
           V    : (HALO 0 -)    (DEC NEG)
           X    : (0 X16)       (DEC NEG)

State XS84 persisting(INF FIN NEG), and arriving (INF FIN NEG):
           PE   : (HALO 0 +)    (DEC NEG)
           KE   : (HALO KE1 -)  (INC NEG)
           VV   : (HALO 0 +)    (INC NEG)
           F    : (HALO 0 -)    (INC NEG)
           A    : (HALO 0 -)    (INC NEG)
           V    : (HALO 0 -)    (DEC NEG)
           X    : (HALO 0 +)    (DEC NEG)

State XS88 persisting(0), and arriving (NEG):
```

E.3. Exaggeration Output

```
PE   : 0              (STD 0)
KE   : KE1            (STD 0)
VV   : (HALO 0 +)     (STD 0)
F    : 0              (INC NEG)
A    : 0              (INC NEG)
V    : (HALO 0 -)     (STD 0)
X    : 0              (DEC NEG)
```

F List of Examples Implemented

This appendix contains a list of examples and the perturbations I used to test DQ analysis and exaggeration. I start with a brief description of the model, present the constaint equations, and list the results for several comparative analysis questions. I state only whether a problem was solved — for space and time reasons the generated explanations cannot be included.

1. **Projectile**

    This is the simplest model of a projectile fired upwards in a uniform gravitational field. I tried several initial conditions: $Y = 0$ and $Y > 0$.

    ```
    (constraints ((d//dt Y V))
                 ((d//dt V G)))
    ```

    - Increased V:
      DQ analysis deduces that rise time increases.
      Exaggeration deduces that rise time increases, max height increases, and fall time increases.
    - Increased G:
      DQ analysis deduces that rise time decreases.
      Exaggeration deduces that rise time decreases, max height decreases, and fall time decreases.

2. **Projectile with Mass**

    ```
    (constraints ((d//dt Y V))
                 ((d//dt V A))
                 ((mult M A F))
                 ((mult M G F)))
    ```

    - Increased V:
      DQ analysis deduces that rise time increases.
      Exaggeration deduces that rise time increases, max height increases, and fall time increases.
    - Increased G:
      DQ analysis deduces that rise time decreases.
      Exaggeration deduces that rise time decreases, max height decreases, and fall time decreases.

- Increased M: Neither DQ analysis or exaggeration deduce anything interesting due to ambiguous qualitative arithmetic.

3. **Projectile with Mass and Energy Conservation**

    NPE means negative potential energy.

    ```
    (constraints ((d//dt Y V))
                 ((d//dt V A))
                 ((mult V V VV))
                 ((mult M VV KE))
                 ((mult Y F NPE))
                 ((add NPE TE KE))
                 ((mult M A F))
                 ((mult M G F)))
    ```

    - Increased V:

        DQ analysis deduces that rise time increases and max height increases.

        Exaggeration deduces that rise time increases, max height increases, and fall time increases.

    - Increased G:

        DQ analysis deduces that rise time decreases.

        Exaggeration deduces that rise time decreases, max height decreases, and fall time decreases.

    - Increased M: Neither DQ analysis or exaggeration deduce anything interesting due to ambiguous qualitative arithmetic.

4. **Projectile with Decreasing Gravity**

    The multiplication constraint says that $A = \frac{G}{Y}$.

    ```
    (constraints ((d//dt Y V))
                 ((d//dt V A))
                 ((mult  Y A G)))
    ```

    - Increased V:

        DQ analysis deduces nothing of interest.

        Exaggeration deduces that rise time increases, max height increases, and fall time increases.

    - Decreased V:

        Exaggeration deduces that rise time decreases, max height decreases, and fall time decreases.

- Increased G:

    DQ analysis deduces nothing of interest.

    Exaggeration deduces nothing conclusively. Simulation is quick but ambiguous — for example, some behaviors take *negl* time to apogee, but some take longer.

- Decreased G:

    Exaggeration deduces that rise time increases and max height increases. It is unable to unambiguously conclude that fall time increases.

5. **Projectile with Decreasing Gravity and Energy Conservation**

```
(constraints ((d//dt Y V))
             ((d//dt V A))
             ((mult V V KE))
             ((mult Y A NPE))
             ((add NPE TE KE))
             ((mult Y A G)))
```

- Increased V:

    DQ analysis deduces that NPE increases at apogee.

    Exaggeration deduces that rise time increases and max height increases.

- Increased G:

    DQ analysis deduces that NPE increases at apogee.

    Exaggeration branches intractably.

6. **Simplest Spring**

    This model is from Kuipers' library. The list of values following the monotonic function constraint is a set of three corresponding values.

```
(constraints ((d//dt X V))
             ((d//dt V A))
             ((M- A X) (0 0) (minf inf) (inf minf)))
```

- Increased X:

    Neither technique deduces anything. In fact, no answer is possible.

7. **Ernie Spring**

   ```
   (constraints ((d//dt X V))
                ((d//dt V A))
                ((mult K-over-M X A)))
   ```

   - Increased K-over-M:
     DQ analysis and exaggeration deduce that the duration (until rest position) decreases.
   - Decreased K-over-M:
     Exaggeration deduces that duration increases.

8. **Standard Spring**

   As with most of the spring models, this was tested with two initial conditions — either position or velocity initially zero. The results listed here are for initial $V = 0$ and $X < 0$.

   ```
   (constraints ((d//dt X V))
                ((d//dt V A))
                ((mult M A F))
                ((mult X K F)))
   ```

   - Increased M:
     DQ analysis and exaggeration deduce that the duration increases.
   - Decreased M:
     DQ analysis and exaggeration deduce that the duration decreases.
   - Increased K:
     DQ analysis and exaggeration deduce that the duration decreases.
   - Decreased K:
     DQ analysis and exaggeration deduces that the duration increases.
   - Increased K and decreased M:
     DQ analysis deduces that the duration decreases.
   - Decreased K and increased M:
     DQ analysis deduces that the duration increases.

- Increased X:

    DQ analysis and exaggeration deduce that max velocity increases:

9. **Spring with Energy Conservation**

```
(constraints ((d//dt X V))
            ((d//dt V A))
            ((mult M A F))
            ((mult X K F))
            ((mult V V VV))
            ((mult VV M KE))
            ((mult F F PE))
            ((add PE KE TE)))
```

- Increased M:

    DQ analysis deduces that the duration of all transition intervals increase, and that max displacement is unchanged.

    Exaggeration deduces that duration increases. With a 50 state limit, HR-QSIM takes 47 seconds to generate several behaviors that are 18 states long.

- Increased K:

    DQ analysis deduces that the duration until first transition decreases, but cannot deduce the other durations because total energy and thus potential energy have increased making it impossible to conclude that the max displacement is unchanged.

    Exaggeration branches intractably.

10. **Linear Pendulum**

    The tests were done with initial conditions that specified dropping the pendulum from an elevated position with zero velocity.

```
(constraints ((d//dt Y V))
            ((d//dt V A))
            ((mult M A FY))
            ((mult F Y FY))
            ((mult M G F)))
```

- Increased M:

    Neither technique deduces anything.

172   Appendix F. List of Examples Implemented

- Increased G:

  DQ analysis and exaggeration deduce that the fall time decreases.

- Decreased G:

  Exaggeration deduces that the fall time increases.

- Increased Y:

  DQ analysis deduces nothing. (This run was done with transition derivative rules inactivated).

- Decreased Y:

  Exaggeration deduces max velocity decreases.

11. **Constant-Coolant Heat Exchanger**

    Hot oil flows through a pipe with velocity V losing heat to a constant temperature coolant surrounding the pipe. Q is oil heat (indistinguishable from temperature), F is heat flow, K is the thermal conductivity of the pipe.

    ```
    (constraints ((d//dt Q F))
                 ((d//dt X V))
                 ((mult K Q F)))
    ```

    - Increased V:

      DQ analysis and exaggeration deduce that the oil spends less time in the exchanger and that the oil exits with more heat.

    - Decreased V:

      Exaggeration deduces that the oil exits slower and cooler,

    - Increased K:

      DQ analysis and exaggeration deduce that the oil loses more heat. The irrelevant-transition filter is essential for exaggeration's success. In addition, DQ analysis concludes that the oil will spend the same time in the exchanger.

    - Decreased K:

      Exaggeration deduces that the oil loses less heat.

    - Increased X:

      DQ analysis and exaggeration deduce that more time is spent in the exchanger and more heat is lost.

- Decreased X:

    Exaggeration deduces that less time is spent and less heat lost.

12. **Warming-Coolant Heat Exchanger**

    In this model, the coolant warms as the hot oil cools. OQ is the heat of the oil, WQ is the heat of the coolant water, F and MF are heat flow and minus heat flow respectively.

    ```
    (constraints ((d//dt OQ F))
                 ((minus F MF))
                 ((d//dt WQ MF))
                 ((d//dt X V))
                 ((add WQ DQ OQ))
                 ((mult K DQ F)))
    ```

    - Increased V:

        DQ analysis deduces only that less time is spent in the exchanger.

        Exaggeration deduces that less time is spent, output oil heat is higher, and water heat is lower.

        DQ analysis deduces only that more time is spent in the exchanger.

    - Increased X:

        Exaggeration deduces that more time is spent and recognizes that oil and water reach thermal equilibrium, but is unable to distinguish this from the *fin* heat change in all the standard behaviors.

    - Decreased X:

        Exaggeration deduces that less time is spent, output oil heat is higher, and water heat is lower.

    - Increased K:

        DQ analysis deduces that duration is unchanged.

        Exaggeration deduces only that *fin* heat is lost in *negl* time, but then branches intractably. Five initial states each reached a 50 state limit producing 181 behaviors.

    - Decreased K:

Exaggeration had no problem. One five state behavior produced. Deduced that less heat was lost by the oil and gained by the water. (Unable to deduce that the time spent in the exchanger was unchanged.)

13. **Walled Heat Exchanger**

    In this model, heat flows from the oil to the pipe wall and then into the water. The two flows have separate thermal conductivity. NET-FLOW is the sum heat flow into the pipe wall.

    ```
    (constraints ((d//dt OQ F1))
                 ((d//dt WQ MF2))
                 ((d//dt PQ NET-FLOW))
                 ((minus F1 MF1))
                 ((minus F2 MF2))
                 ((add MF1 F2 NET-FLOW))
                 ((add PQ DQ1 OQ))
                 ((add WQ DQ2 PQ))
                 ((mult K1 DQ1 F1))
                 ((mult K2 DQ2 F2))
                 ((d//dt X V)))
    ```

    - Increased V:
      DQ analysis deduces that duration is decreased.
      Exaggeration deduces that duration is decreased, output oil heat is increased, water heat is decreased, and pipe heat is decreased.
    - Increased K1 and increased K2:
      DQ analysis deduces that duration is unchanged.
      Exaggeration branches intractably.
    - Decreased K1 and decreased K2:
      Exaggeration still branches intractably—with a 500 state limit HR-QSIM generates 325 behaviors that are 9 states long and X does not pass $\prec x_0, 0 \succ$. The problem is that NET-FLOW can keep changing HR-QDIR.

14. **Double Flow Heat Exchanger**

    This is a modification the heat exchanger in which two 'substances' are being exchanged: heat (Q) and danger (D). This example was defined primarily to test the DQ analysis topological code.

```
(constraints ((d//dt Q F))
             ((d//dt X V))
             ((mult K Q F))
             ((d//dt D E))
             ((mult C D E)))
```

- Increased V:

    DQ analysis and exaggeration deduce that duration is decreased, output heat is increased, and output danger is increased.

15. **Super-Heated Boiler**

    This is a rather inaccurate model of a boiler connected to a steam superheater in series. The chief question is what happens to the steam output temperature when warmer water is presented to the boiler? DQ analysis correctly answers that the steam will cool down since the boiling rate (Rb) will increase causing more steam to compete for the superheater's heat. See [3] for a better model of this system.

    The list (212 0 212) is a set of corresponding values that the add constraint must obey.

```
(constraints ((add Ti deltaT Tboil) (212 0 212))
             ((mult Rb deltaT Fb))
             ((d//dt X Rb))
             ((d//dt Ts Fs)))
```

- Increased Ti:

    DQ analysis deduces that the boiling rate increases, and the output temperature of the steam decreases.

16. **Two Transitions**

    This model was used to test the DQ analysis topology algorithm.

```
(constraints ((d//dt A D))
             ((d//dt B D)))
```

17. **Three Transitions**

    This model was used to test the DQ analysis topology algorithm.

```
(constraints ((d//dt A DA))
             ((d//dt B DB))
             ((d//dt C DC)))
```

18. **Fragmenting Three**

    This model was used to test the DQ analysis topology algorithm. In one behavior, three parameters transition at once, but by perturbing D, they can be forced to all split apart.

```
(constraints ((d//dt A D))
             ((d//dt B MD))
             ((d//dt C CD))
             ((mult D MD ONE)))
```

19. **Pumped Containers**

    See section 4.3.2 for a discussion of this model. The DQ analysis explanation is very nice. La and Lb are the fluid levels of containers A and B, H is the height difference, Fp is the pumped flow, Fs is the seeping flow, and Fn is the net flow.

```
(constraints ((minus La Lb))
             ((add Lb H La))
             ((add Fp Fs Fn))
             ((mult H PERMIABILITY Fs))
             ((d//dt La Fn)))
```

- Increased Fp:

  DQ analysis deduces that equilibrium height and seeping flow are increased.

  Exaggeration deduces that the equilibrium height, level in A, and seeping flow are increased while the level in B is decreased.

- Increased PERMIABILITY:

  DQ analysis deduces that the equilibrium seeping flow is unchanged (since it is equal to pumped flow) thus height is decreased.

  Exaggeration deduces that height and the level in A are decreased while the level in B is increased.

20. **Series RC Circuit**

    Close a circuit to charge a capacitor hooked in series with a resistor.

```
(constraints ((D//dt Vc dVc))
             ((add Vr Vc V))
             ((mult R I Vr))
             ((mult C dVc I)))
```

- Increased C:

  DQ analysis and exaggeration deduce that it takes longer to charge the capacitor.

- Increased R:

  DQ analysis and exaggeration deduce that it takes longer because the current is smaller.

- Increased V:

  DQ analysis and exaggeration deduce nothing of great interest.

21. **Parallel RC Circuit**

    See [70, p350] for a description of this circuit.

```
(constraints ((mult R Ir V))
             ((minus Ir Ic))
             ((D//dt V dv))
             ((mult dV C Ic)))
```

- Increase R:

  DQ analysis and exaggeration deduce that it takes longer for the capacitor to discharge.

- Increase V:

  Neither technique deduces anything interesting.

- Increase C:

  DQ analysis and exaggeration deduce that it takes longer for the capacitor to discharge.

22. **Two RC Series Circuits in Parallel**

```
(constraints ((D//dt Vc1 dVc1))
             ((D//dt Vc2 dVc2))
             ((add Vr1 Vc1 V))
             ((add Vr2 Vc2 V))
             ((mult R1 I1 Vr1))
             ((mult R2 I2 Vr2))
             ((mult C1 dVc1 I1))
             ((mult C2 dVc2 I2))
             ((add I1 I2 I)))
```

- Increase R2:

    DQ analysis deduces that the time to charge C2 will increase, but that the time to charge C1 won't change.

    Exaggeration deduces that it will take longer to charge C2.

- Decrease C2:

    DQ analysis deduces that the time to charge C2 will decrease, but that the time to charge C1 won't change.

    Exaggeration deduces nothing of interest.

Bibliography

[1] S. Addanki, R. Cremonini, and J. S. Penberthy. Reasoning about Assumptions in Graphs of Models. In *Proceedings of IJCAI-89*, August 1989.

[2] L. Chua and P. Lin. *Computer Aided Analysis of Electronic Circuits: Algorithms and Techniques*. Prentice Hall, Englewood Cliffs, NJ, 1975.

[3] J. Collins and K. Forbus. Reasoning About Fluids Via Molecular Collections. In *Proceedings of AAAI-87*, July 1987.

[4] E. Davis. Order of Magnitude Reasoning in Qualitative Differential Equations. Technical Report 312, NYU Computer Science Department, August 1987.

[5] M. Davis and R. Hersh. Nonstandard Analysis. *Scientific American*, June 1972.

[6] R. Davis. Diagnostic Reasoning Based on Structure and Behavior. *Aritificial Intelligence*, 24, 1984.

[7] R. Davis and W. Hamscher. Model Based Reasoning: Troubleshooting. In *Exploring Artificial Intelligence*, pages 297–346. Morgan Kaufmann, 1988.

[8] J. de Kleer. Qualitative and Quantitative Knowledge in Classical Mechanics. Ai-tr-352, MIT AI Lab, December 1975.

[9] J. de Kleer. Causal and Teleological Reasoning in Circuit Recognition. Ai-tr-529, MIT AI Lab, September 1979.

[10] J. de Kleer. How Circuits Work. *Artificial Intelligence*, 24, December 1984.

[11] J. de Kleer and J. Brown. A Qualitative Physics Based on Confluences. *Artificial Intelligence*, 24, December 1984.

[12] J. de Kleer, J. Doyle, G. L. Steele, and G. J. Sussman. AMORD: Explicit Control of Reasoning. In *Proceedings of the Symposium on Artificial Intelligence and Programming Languages*, Rochester, N.Y., August 1977. SIGART.

[13] J. de Kleer and G. Sussman. Propagation of Constraints Applied to Circuit Synthesis. Aim-485, MIT AI Lab, 1978.

[14] J. de Kleer and B. Williams. Back to Backtracking: Controlling the ATMS. In *Procceedings of the AAAI*, August 1986.

[15] J. de Kleer and B. Williams. Diagnosing Multiple Faults. *Artificial Intelligence*, 32, April 1987.

[16] G. DeJong and R. Mooney. Explanation-Based Learning: An Alternative View. *Machine Learning*, 1(2), 1986.

[17] J. Dormoy and O. Raiman. Assembling a Device. In *Proceedings of AAAI-88*, pages 330–335, August 1988.

[18] J. Dormoy and O. Raiman. Assembling a Device. *International Journal for Artificial Intelligence in Engineering*, pages 216–226, October 1988.

[19] H. Enderton. *A Mathematical Introduction to Logic*. Academic Press, New York, NY, 1972.

[20] B. Falkenhainer and K. Forbus. Setting up Large Scale Qualitative Models. In *Proceedings of AAAI-88*, August 1988.

[21] K. Forbus. Qualitative Process Theory. *Artificial Intelligence*, 24, December 1984.

[22] K. Forbus. The Logic of Occurrence. In *Proceedings of IJCAI-87*, pages 409–415, August 1987.

[23] K. Forbus. Qualitative Physics: Past, Present, and Future. In *Exploring Artificial Intelligence*, pages 239–296. Morgan Kaufmann, 1988.

[24] K. Forbus. Introducing Actions into Qualitative Simulation. In *Proceedings IJCAI-89*, pages 1273–1278, August 1989.

[25] K. Forbus. The Qualitative Process Engine. In *Readings in Qualitative Reasoning about Physical Systems*, pages 220–235. Morgan Kaufmann, August 1989.

[26] K. Forbus and A. Stevens. Using Qualitative Simulation to Generate Explanations. Technical Report 4490, Bolt Beranek and Newman Inc, March 1981.

[27] W. Hamscher and R. Davis. Issues in Diagnosis from First Principles. AI Memo 893, MIT AI Lab, March 1987.

[28] S. Hanks. Representing and Computing Temporally Scoped Beliefs. In *Proceedings of AAAI-88*, August 1988.

[29] S. Hanks. Projecting Plans about Uncertain Worlds. Ph.D. Thesis, Yale University Computer Science Department, Forthcoming 1990.

[30] P. Hayes. Naive Physics I: Ontology for Liquids. In *Formal Theories of the Commonsense World*. Ablex, 1985.

[31] P. Hayes. The Second Naive Physics Manifesto. In *Formal Theories of the Commonsense World*. Ablex, 1985.

[32] J. Henle and E. Kleinberg. *Infinitesimal Calculus*. The MIT Press, Cambridge, 1979.

[33] Y. Iwasaki and H. Simon. Causality In Device Dehavior. *Artificial Intelligence*, 29(1):3–32, July 1986.

[34] S. Kedar-Cabelli and L. McCarthy. Explanation-Based Generalization as Resolution Theorem Proving. In *Proceedings of the Fourth International Workshop on Machine Learning*, Irvine, CA, June 1987.

[35] J. Keisler. *Foundations of Infinitessimal Calculus*. Prindle, Webber and Schmidt, Inc., Boston, 1976.

[36] B. Kuipers. Getting the Envisionment Right. In *Proceedings of AAAI-82*, August 1982.

[37] B. Kuipers. The Limits of Qualitative Simulation. In *Proceedings of IJCAI-85*, August 1985.

[38] B. Kuipers. Qualitative Simulation. *Artificial Intelligence*, 29, September 1986.

Bibliography

[39] B. Kuipers. Abstraction by Time-Scale in Qualitative Simulation. In *Proceedings of AAAI-87*, July 1987.

[40] B. Kuipers and C. Chiu. Taming Intractable Branching in Qualitative Simulation. In *Proceedings of IJCAI-87*, August 1987.

[41] T. Mitchell, R. Keller, and S. Kedar-Cabelli. Explanation-Based Generalization: A Unifying View. *Machine Learning*, 1(1), 1986.

[42] J. Moses. Algebraic Simplification: A Guide for the Perplexed. *Communications of the ACM*, 14(8), August 1971.

[43] J. R. Munkres. *Topology, A First Course*. Prentice-Hall, Inc., Englewood Cliffs, NJ, 1975.

[44] S. Murthy and S. Addanki. PROMPT: An Innovative Design Tool. In *Proceedings of AAAI-87*, pages 637–642, August 1987.

[45] R. Patil. Causal Representation of Patient Illness for Electrolyte and Acid-Base Diagnosis. TR-267, MIT Laboratory for Computer Science, October 1981.

[46] J. Pearl. *Probablistic Reasoning in Intelligent Systems*. Morgan Kaufmann, San Mateo, CA, 1988.

[47] J.S. Penberthy. Incremental Analysis and the Graph of Models: A First Step towards Analysis in the Plumber's World. MS Thesis, MIT Laboratory for Computer Science, January 1987.

[48] O. Raiman. Order of Magnitude Reasoning. In *Proceedings of AAAI-86*, August 1986.

[49] A. Robinson. *Non-Standard Analysis*. North-Holland Publishing Company, Amsterdam, 1966.

[50] W. Rudin. *Principles of Mathematical Analysis, third edition*. McGraw-Hill Book Company, New York, 1976.

[51] E. Sacks. Qualitative Mathematical Reasoning. In *Proceedings of IJCAI-85*, pages 137–139, August 1985.

[52] E. Sacks. Piecewise Linear Reasoning. In *Proceedings of AAAI-87*, pages 655–659, August 1987.

[53] E. Sacks. Automatic Qualitative Analysis of Ordinary Differential Equations Using Piecewise Linear Approximations. Phd thesis, Massachusetts Institute of Technology, February 1988.

[54] P. Samuelson. *Foundations of Economic Analysis*. Harvard University Press, Cambridge, MA, 1947.

[55] E. Sandewall. Filter Preferential Entailment for the Logic of Actions in Almost Continuous Worlds. In *Proceedings IJCAI-89*, pages 894–899, August 1989.

[56] J. Shearer, A. Murphy, and Richardson H. *Introduction to System Dynamics*. Addison-Wesley Publishing Company, Reading, MA, 1971.

[57] Y. Shoham. Reasoning about Change: Time and Causation from the Standpoint of Artificial Intelligence. YALEU/CSD/RR#507, Yale University Computer Science Department, December 1986.

[58] R. Simmons. "Commonsense" Arithmetic Reasoning. In *Proceedings of AAAI-86*, pages 118–124, August 1986.

[59] G. Skorstad and K. Forbus. Qualitative and Quantitative Reasoning about Thermodynamics. In *Proceedings of the Tenth Annual Conference of the Cognitive Science Society*, August 1989.

[60] P. Struss. Mathematical Aspects of Qualitative Reasoning. *International Journal for Artificial Intelligence in Engineering*, 3(3), July 1988.

[61] G.J. Sussman and G.L. Steele. CONSTRAINTS: A Language for Expressing Almost-Hierarchical Descriptions. *Artificial Intelligence*, 14:1–39, 1980.

[62] D. Weld. Explaining Complex Engineered Devices. Technical Report 5489, Bolt Beranek and Newman Inc, November 1983.

[63] D. Weld. Combining Discrete and Continuous Process Models. In *Proceedings of IJCAI-85*, 1985.

[64] D. Weld. The Use of Aggregation in Causal Simulation. *Artificial Intelligence*, 30(1), October 1986.

[65] D. Weld. Comparative Analysis. In *Proceedings of IJCAI-87*, August 1987.

[66] D. Weld. Choices for Comparative Analysis: DQ Analysis or Exaggeration? *International Journal for Artificial Intelligence in Engineering*, 3(3), July 1988.

[67] D. Weld. Automated Model Switching. Technical Report 89-08-01, University of Washington, Department of Computer Science and Engineering, October 1989.

[68] D. Weld and J. de Kleer, editors. *Readings in Qualitative Reasoning about Physical Systems*. Morgan Kaufmann, San Mateo, CA, August 1989.

[69] B. Williams. Qualitative Analysis of MOS Circuits. *Artificial Intelligence*, December 1984.

[70] B. Williams. The Role of Continuity in a Qualitative Physics. In *Proceedings of AAAI-84*, August 1984.

[71] B. Williams. Principled Design Based on Qualitative Behavioral Descriptions. Phd thesis proposal, MIT Artifical Intelligence Lab, November 1985.

[72] B. Williams. Doing Time: Putting Qualitative Reasoning on Firmer Ground. In *Proceedings of AAAI-86*, pages 105–112, August 1986.

[73] B. Williams. Exorcising Control of Demon Invocation: A Study in Tractable Non-Monotonicity. AI Memo 944, MIT Artificial Intelligence Lab, 1987.

[74] B. Williams. MINIMA: A Symbolic Approach to Qualitative Algebraic Reasoning. In *Proceedings of AAAI-88*, August 1988.

Index

ABEL, 141
aggregation, 141
algebraic reasoning, 107, 114–115, 138
ambiguity, 15, 46, 51, 102, <u>105</u>, 107, 140
AMORD, 45
approximation reformulations, 142
Archimedian principle, 62
ARK, 45, 47
asymptotic values, 111
behavior generation, 12
behavior, 13, <u>31</u>
 hyperreal, 66
boiler, 71
CA, 45
CHEPACHET, 133
closed, 75
CO-transition, 76
compacting, 58
compactness theorem, 63
 inter-model, 14, 141
 non-differential, 14, 67, 138
comparative statics, 128
completeness, 114
comuptational complexity, 116
consider assumptions, 142
constraint filters, 82
continuity, 73, 75
corresponding values, 82
derivative constraint, 82
 interval, <u>40</u>, 48
 transition, <u>41</u>
design, 7
device ontology, 10
diagnosis, 7, 48
differential qualitative analysis, 15, <u>29</u>
 in qualitative process theory, 130
discontinuous systems, 139
distance, 89
distance-by, 37
distance-rate-time table, 87, 107
distinguished time point, <u>30</u>, 66
duration rule, <u>37</u>, 48, 108, 130
 converse, 49
 end of time rule, <u>44</u>
envisionment, 12, 133
EQUAL, 5
exaggeration, 20, <u>61</u>
explanation based generalization, 47
explanation quality, 119
FOG, 130
graph of models, 141
halo, 24, 64
heat exchanger, 19, 50, 61, 134

counter-flow, 67
history generation, 12, 128
hyperreal numbers, 23, <u>64</u>
I-transition, 76
incremental qualitative analysis, 129
infinite number, 65
infinite-distance arrival rule, 93, 107, 134
infinitesimal number, 65
intelligent tutoring systems, 8
intermediate value theorem, 77
interval constant rule, <u>43</u>, 48
irrelevant-transition filter, 96
kidney, 132
landmark value, 9, <u>30</u>, 64
 new, 13
least-upper bound property, 84
lineraity, 107
linguistic variables, 9
Macsyma, 5
magnitude semantics, 33
mean value theorem, 77
model-switching, 142
monotonicity, 110, 112
multiplication rule, <u>44</u>, 48
nonstandard analysis, 23, 62, 131, <u>153</u>
NS-transition, 78
OC-transition, 76
one's own derivative rule, <u>44</u>
open, 75
order topology, 75
P-transition, 76
parameter, <u>29</u>
parameter-change rule, 141
partial derivatives, 109
persistence, 25
perspective, 15
 time as, 130
 covering, <u>34</u>
 none, 108
 partial, <u>34</u>
 time as, 35
perspective-flipping rule, <u>42</u>, 47
piecewise linear approximations, 127
predecessor-persistence filtering, 25, <u>84</u>, 134
process ontology, 11
projectile, 101
PROMPT, 141
pumped flow, 116
QSIM, 12–13, 45, 51, 64, <u>73</u>, 106
QUAL, 5, 129
qualitative direction, <u>30</u>, 64–65
qualitative hyperreal representation, 24

qualitative physics, 4
qualitative process theory, 9, 11, 130
qualitative resolution rule, 107
qualitative state, <u>30</u>
qualitative value, <u>30</u>, 64
quantity lattice, 142
quantity space, 9
reasonable function, 29, 64
relative change value, 15, 141
 interval, <u>34</u>
relative change, <u>32</u>
SAM, 141
scale phase, 22, <u>98</u>, 111
SCHISM, 6
self-reference rule, <u>42</u>, 48
sensitivity analysis, 127
signed semantics, 33
simplifying assumptions, 141
simulate phase, 21, <u>72</u>
slices, 6
SN-transition, 78
soundness, 113
splitting, 59
spring/block system, 15, 33, 45, 159
stalling, 59
starting, 59
state tree, 51
structural description, 30
successor-arrival filtering, 25, <u>89</u>, 134
successor-arrival time, 25
SYN, 5
system, <u>30</u>
temporal continuity rule, 96
temporal projection, 12
temporal topology rule, 133
time function, <u>31</u>
time scale abstraction, 132
time-scale abstraction, 141
topological equality, <u>32</u>, 38, 49
transform phase, 21, <u>67</u>
transition constant rule, <u>43</u>
transition table, 73
transition, <u>31</u>, 66
variance, 134
Waltz filtering, 74, 82
width, 86

ARTIFICIAL INTELLIGENCE

Patrick Henry Winston and J. Michael Brady, founding editors
J. Michael Brady, Daniel G. Bobrow, and Randall Davis, current editors

Artificial Intelligence: An MIT Perspective, Volume I: Expert Problem Solving, Natural Language Understanding, Intelligent Computer Coaches, Representation and Learning, edited by Patrick Henry Winston and Richard Henry Brown, 1979

Artificial Intelligence: An MIT Perspective, Volume II: Understanding Vision, Manipulation, Computer Design, Symbol Manipulation, edited by Patrick Henry Winston and Richard Henry Brown, 1979

NETL: A System for Representing and Using Real-World Knowledge, Scott Fahlman, 1979

The Interpretation of Visual Motion, by Shimon Ullman, 1979

A Theory of Syntactic Recognition for Natural Language, Mitchell P. Marcus, 1980

Turtle Geometry: The Computer as a Medium for Exploring Mathematics, Harold Abelson and Andrea di Sessa, 1981

From Images to Surfaces: A Computational Study of the Human Visual System, William Eric Leifur Grimson, 1981

Robot Manipulators: Mathematics, Programming, and Control, Richard P. Paul, 1981

Computational Models of Discourse, edited by Michael Brady and Robert C. Berwick, 1982

Robot Motion: Planning and Control, edited by Michael Brady, John M. Hollerbach, Timothy Johnson, Tomás Lozano-Pérez, and Matthew T. Mason, 1982

In-Depth Understanding : A Computer Model of Integrated Processing for Narrative Comprehension, Michael G. Dyer, 1983

Robotic Research: The First International Symposium, edited by Hideo Hanafusa and Hirochika Inoue, 1985

Robot Hands and the Mechanics of Manipulation, Matthew T. Mason and J. Kenneth Salisbury, Jr., 1985

The Acquisition of Syntactic Knowledge, Robert C. Berwick, 1985

The Connection Machine, W. Daniel Hillis, 1985

Legged Robots that Balance, Marc H. Raibert, 1986

Robotics Research: The Third International Symposium, edited by O.D. Faugeras and Georges Giralt, 1986

Machine Interpretation of Line Drawings, Kokichi Sugihara, 1986

ACTORS: A Model of Concurrent Computation in Distributed Systems, Gul A. Agha, 1986

Knowledge-Based Tutoring: The GUIDON Program, William Clancey, 1987

AI in the 1980s and Beyond: An MIT Survey, edited by W. Eric L. Grimson and Ramesh S. Patil, 1987

Visual Reconstruction, Andrew Blake and Andrew Zisserman, 1987

Reasoning about Change: Time and Causation from the Standpoint of Artificial Intelligence, Yoav Shoham, 1988

Model-Based Control of a Robot Manipulator, Chae H. An, Christopher G. Atkeson, and John M. Hollerbach, 1988

A Robot Ping-Pong Player: Experiment in Real-Time Intelligent Control, Russell L. Andersson, 1988

Robotics Research: The Fourth International Symposium, edited by Robert C. Bolles and Bernard Roth, 1988

The Paralation Model: Architecture-Independent Parallel Programming, Gary Sabot, 1988

Concurrent System for Knowledge Processing: An Actor Perspective, edited by Carl Hewitt and Gul Agha, 1989

Automated Deduction in Nonclassical Logics: Efficient Matrix Proof Methods for Modal and Intuitionistic Logics, Lincoln Wallen, 1989

3D Model Recognition from Stereoscopic Cues, edited by John E.W. Mayhew and John P. Frisby, 1989

Shape from Shading, edited by Berthold K.P. Horn and Michael J. Brooks, 1989

Ontic: A Knowledge Representation System for Mathematics, David A. McAllester, 1989

Automated Proof Search in Non-Classical Logics: Efficient Matrix Proof Methods for Modal and Intuitionistic Logics, Lincoln A. Wallen, 1989

Solid Shape, Jan J. Koenderink, 1990

Theories of Comparative Analysis, Daniel S. Weld, 1990

JUL 3 0 1990